PLAY THAT GAME
Bojan Mladenović

playthatgame-book.com

Writings and materials related to certain historical events and personalities were used in this novel. The purpose of this novel is not to belittle or offend anyone, but solely to educate and entertain.

The content of the novel represents the artistic expression of the author.

Bojan Mladenović

Play That Game

Let the business be your playground

Table of Contents

Foreword 9
Let's Begin 15
It's All Just a Game 18
Identification 24
There is no I in the Team 26
The Goal Philosophy 29
Stay in Your Own Lane 32
Are We on the Same Page? 37
The Ease of Walking Away 40
The Road to Success 44
Living Mechanism 48
Burnout Syndrome 54
The Best of What You Have 57
Loyalty 60
Focus on the Team 63
Empathy 67
Journey 70
Moderation 74
Active Listening 77
Bad Transfer 81
Negative Selection 85
Think 87
Dirty Dancing 93
Cause and Effect 95
Focus 98
Until the Last Whistle 100
Surprise Factor 103
Everything is Visible 106
Productivity 108
Benefits 112
Behind the Scenes 115
Shortsightedness 119
I Came with a Purpose 122

The Impostor Syndrome 124
Two-way Street..128
A Guy for Everything 130
Out of Sight, Out of Mind...................................134
Onboarding 138
Far Away from Here..141
Work Begets Work, and Idleness Begets Idleness 145
Inevitability of Improvement..............................147
Unlearning 150
Until You Make It..154
Process and Progress...161
Inspirer 167
Giants..172
Silver Bullet 176
In the end 181
Afterword..182

'If I have seen further than others, it is by standing on the shoulders of giants.'

Sir Isaac Newton

Foreword

ojan Mladenovic has written an excellent novel, even though he would never agree on the term novel. It brings the traits of 20th century American literature into our own. He speaks about business, its development in the modern world, and life philosophy through the prism of practical examples taken from the world of sport. You might not have given it a thought but a successful coach, manager or an athlete can be an example of a success in the world of business in which team spirit, motivation and risk management skills are highly valued.

This idea that sports teams, coaches, managers and athletes should be perceived as successful business world representatives might sound a bit funny at first but the truth is that they have quite a lot in common with acknowledged business leaders and entrepreneurs.

Apart from the aforementioned skills, sports can serve as the source of a myriad of life philosophies.

Persistence and mental stamina are the prerequisites for achieving success in sports. However, they are necessary traits for developing resilience and endurance in the world of business. Sport can help develop ethical values such as respect for the opponent and honor, which are essential for achieving success.

All things considered, sport can be viewed as an invaluable asset for example of developing skills and characteristics needed for achieving success in the world of business, and Bojan Mladenovic's novel nourishes this way of thinking.

Learning from a personal experience is important just as is asking for other people's advice. Regardless of the decades of experience behind you, there are people who are more experienced and more knowledgeable and who have perspectives which you can find useful for your own business style. You need to bear in mind, though, whose advice you decide to follow so that you could avoid potential mistakes and wrong decisions. There is a saying in the southern parts of Serbia *'Listen to the elders but don't follow them'*. It means that it is important to be open to novelty and continuous education and development, but following the bottomup principle, ultimately decide on your own path. This is something that has been passed down for generations in my family as words of wisdom.

As a person with decades of experience in the public domain, privatelyowned businesses, both small and largescale, and multinational companies, Bojan Mladenovic shares with us his viewpoint, being the elderly from the saying, the old wise sage, and tells us the following,

'Children, I'm leaving this with you, all my knowledge and experience gained, and you decide what you'll make of it...' And that is where the true value of this book lies. In an interesting and comprehensible way, Bojan Mladenovic offers his viewpoint and his experience to us as guidelines on the realistic state of things, which might not mean much to the Google Maps generations, opposing, in that way, the inadequately updated app data.

'Play That Game' might not even be a novel (here I stand corrected) but an experiment of a kind of a successful business manager not to become a renowned writer but to attempt to demystify modern business world so that newbies, as well as the experienced players, could see, think about and then decide what to do to tackle the daily challenges.

Does this sound intriguing? I would say it is rather useful for everyone who wants to understand the business world and the ways of dealing with the challenges it poses on a daily basis. This book might be helpful to novices and experienced players alike; even to the ones who do not play that game but would love to learn more about it.

Demystifying the world of business can be the key to success since some people cannot face the obstacles and challenges, which prevents them from making progress. Books such as this one can provide practical advice and strategies for overcoming such obstacles thus helping people to become successful in their endeavors.

Since this book is about business, I think that those who want to expand their knowledge and understanding of the ways that world functions will find it invaluable, regardless of their experience in the field.

To wrap it up, the last thing to say about the 'Play that Game' novel is *'Let the games begin...'*

Milos Grozdanovic,
a writer and the editor of the book

Play That Game

Let's Begin

Inspired by true events. I've always loved the movies that begin with this line, be it true or not. It makes the whole thing more believable, giving us hope that somebody really went through the ordeal described in the plot line. If anything, it is a marketing strategy hitting the bullseye.

However, this has nothing to do with marketing…I guess you know the feeling: you have five Google accounts opened for the needs of the companies you have worked for, approximately 17 notepads which you used to jot down all the necessary pieces of information to preserve them from oblivion, scribbled ideas, thoughts and concepts. Million different notepads in your private or company phones that have previously been used. Not to mention the multitude of files on stick memories, hard discs, CDs or even, in my case, floppy discs. Yes, I am **that** generation. All the print screens on the mobile phones and the saved photos which ended up God knows where. And when you remembered something that would be a nice addition to a business idea, a confirmation that you are on the right track, something that is worth remembering or worth passing on to your children as words of wisdom learnt from the source, which would be priceless at that moment, and when you know that you need all of that at that particular moment or you will forget those important things shortly afterwards, then you make a reminder of the things to be reminded of.

That's the reason I've decided to write this down. To have everything in one place so that I will eventually be spared of the endless search for its fragments in the future. One evening I started writing with the idea that it would be liberating. Having finished twenty pages, I realized that I would need to systematize so much more. At that point I said to myself that it would be quite a workload. And I don't even like writing! Some would argue that writing could be a form of therapy. So, I definitely should give it a try. It might mean to me. And, while writing, I actually realized that it might also mean to somebody else. Why not! It should be continued once it was set into motion. And to be honest, I'm writing all this as a reminder to myself and my children of everything that I have said to them or wanted to say but have never had the chance.

Despite all the creativity and love for sci-fi present in my personality, it is the rational part of my being that has brought stability to my daily functioning. Standing firm on our own two feet, we fight against ourselves and the world. Everything is based on emotions; we are living organisms. We are humans. Emotions do exist in business but they should have no say in the decisionmaking process. Our lives will be so much easier if we learn not just from our own and other people's experience but from the wisdom of the people who actually have something to say. It is true that the most common and the best way is to learn from one's own mistakes, but we all know that it is without a doubt the most painful way, too. Who we learn from also matters since it might accelerate us towards the truth and rightdoing. Having bad mentors can lead us astray, which can have a detrimental effect on our future and life. However, even that is a learning opportunity. Recently, I've learnt that Sir Alex Ferguson's opus is taught at Economics at Harvard University. I literally learnt that when I finished writing so I took it as a sign of my being on the right track.

Given the fact that I'm a huge sports fan, of football in particular, I created an analogy which enabled me to have a better perspective of all the challenges a football team, or a company, and the players, that is, employees and managers, are faced with on a daily basis. All the strategies of managing the company, its teams and employees that deserve special attention, consideration and adaptation to new situations, need understanding. In that way, it was easier for me to comprehend everything that was going on in the rough world of the ruthless market. I needed to demystify it all so that I could have the clarity of vision from which I would decide what to do next to face all the challenges of each day.

Welcome to my world.

It's All Just a Game

It's a perfect time for a break. It's raining outside, which is great. This rain would bore everyone to death. But I need such rain right now. A long aimless walk has always done me good, and this drizzle is ideal for cooling off and resetting for the end of the day.

When I think a bit more about it, nothing is aimless, not even this walk. Every activity, as futile as it may seem, has its beginning, its end and, naturally, its purpose. Burning calories, stress relieving, thought gathering…a standard walking route by the river, preferably without any conversation. Just walking and nothing more! Try as I might to succeed in achieving such lonesome walks, I have always failed to do that. Man is a social being. Even though he sometimes seeks solitude, he feels more pleasant in the presence of others. The decision has been made. The plan has been created. A brisk walk by the river, just to get what's left of my hair wet, and then off to a local café.

The local café is a truthfully wonderful place. It's thematically elfishly decorated, with the largest number of sports fanatics in one place. It's amazing how many local guys follow and comment on absolutely every sports event there is. Football, basketball, tennis… Luckily, we have always had our favorite to root for. National teams, clubs. And if we didn't have a favorite to root for, we would always have somebody to be against. The place has always been crowded. Its visitors have been interesting people of different levels of education, from high school leavers to doctorate degree holders. Astonishingly enough, they are all connected by the same passion for sport which provides them with the abundance of opportunity for the most incredible conversations, discussions about players, strategies and result outcomes.

It is absolutely amazing that nowadays you can have a heated conversation full of opposing competitive rivalry reaching its climax on the verge of a conflict, only to end with each side holding firmly onto their convictions and having a pint as if nothing happened.

Yes, that's what I'll do. I'll take a stroll by the river, get wet in the rain, but not too much to have to change, and go to the café for a pint because vitamin B is beneficial for your health, sleep and mental focus. This has been said so many times that I've finally started believing in it. The force of selfconviction is the most potent one.

The new Premier League season is about to start. It is an inexhaustible source of conversation. What kind of tactic is each team going to use? Who is the main favorite for the title? Who are the most likely drop outs? And naturally, which team got the best reinforcements during the transfer period? That League is, in my opinion, the absolute winner among all other European leagues.

I've always liked the Premier League and it is not because of the quality of the game or the number of scored goals. I like it because of the honor. The players play honorably, they are tough, without any pretense or fake falls or simulations. When and if some of those appeared, the players themselves would deal with the fakers. It is beneath them to simulate. It has always been, even until this very day, the one and only genuine league and honor is the reason for it, the foundation upon which it was built. When the foundation is solid and healthy, and you know you are doing the right thing, success comes as something inevitable. Since the day the League was founded, each team has received the same treatment, financially speaking, from the basic things such as TV rights, which led to healthy competition among the teams which again, in turn, brought about the quality. Unlike other European leagues (Spanish, Italian, German, etc.) which have always privileged two or three teams over others, in this League the nucleus is made up of six or ten teams. This is the League in which the second league newcomers managed to win the title. It has always been a true inspiration to watch and enjoy. Incessant fight for each and every ball until the end of the match. Chivalry at its best.

An accompanying event to the Premier League is the Fantasy Premier League. It has been developed as a game about the game, that is, a game within the game. Every Fantasy Premier League player can create his own football team in the world of fantasy, and the results of the team depend on the results that the chosen players achieve in real life. Complicated, eh? Not really, just addictive for the ones who like football and even more so for the ones who are keen on analytics. When I discovered it, I got hooked on it. My goal was to become the best manager in the fantasy world. Some people like sudoku or crossword puzzles. As for myself and some other ten million active players worldwide, Fantasy is unsurpassed for now. Although, sometimes it can ruin the real game.

I have always been a gamer and I have always had a positive take on that one. Why? To start with, my generation developed its motor ability for jaywalking by playing the famous 'Frogger' game. The frog that crosses the street in the game had a significant influence on the accurate, or even better, timely good decision making. Can it be linked to entrepreneurship? To what extent does driving simulation positively affect passing the driving license test? Not to mention the flight simulations…

The evolution in game development initiated my wish to organize. It started with playing strategies. Creating civilizations, waging wars, preserving the economy and people's welfare, allocating resources, investing… sounds familiar? Management? Have young entrepreneurs been selected by their successfulness in the virtual world? I don't think so. I believe that everyone eventually finds what they have been looking for, and I have always wanted to organize, lead, create. You get second chances in the virtual world, but the question is do you get those in the real one? It is possible, of course, to get a second chance. After all, we get as many chances as we allow ourselves. Games serve as a testing ground without real casualties. They are simply simulations of economic, sports or war events sans consequences, enabling us to fight in the virtual arena, to test ourselves. Does it come with a price? Naturally. The excess of anything, food, drinks, women, water, even games, is a bad thing. You lose your touch with reality. But in reasonable amounts it can only be useful. What is equally important is the choice of the games that a person plays. Similar choices matter in real life: the books that a person reads, the music they listen or the people they hang out with. They do matter. If you choose to do the right thing, you also need to do it in the right way. It has always been important, as it always will be, which wolf you choose to feed.

The beauty lies in having the possibility to choose. I say beauty, even though 'privilege' is more to the point. Or is it just an illusion? The real question is whether we can have our say in it or it is just the privilege that a minority have. I'd say the latter. And the minority was not given that privilege but it asked for it and got it. 'Ask and it will be given to you; seek, and you will find; knock, and it will be opened to you.' Now this sounds familiar. Luke 11, 9-10. Unless you ask for a chance, you will never get it.

Sounds funny? It is not. Neither is it complicated. It is quite simple, really. If you don't get a chance, then create one for yourself. Just like in sports. Your opponent is better? In what ways? His physical readiness? Then you should start working on your own and you yourself will be better. Strategy? Study hard and you will be more knowledgeable. Need a chance? Create it! It's simple. No more excuses. You can always find the solution to your problem. And if there is none, well then, that's the solution, too.

To go back to the Fantasy Premier League of England. I love English football, and two things in particular, analytics and management. In my virtual world, I choose my team. I make my own decisions based on my own perception and the players' success in real life. Analytical data are my wordsearch quizzes, my passion, my fetish. Is it fun? It is to me! Is it useful? Well, my brain is always active. Some say that such brain activity is good for Alzheimer's disease prevention. It's a winwin situation, thank you very much. In my opinion all the necessary prerequisites for the further development of my Fantasy team have been met. Does it get boring over time? Yes, it does for a second, but the point is that there are a few million lunatics like me in the world, at least 50 in my neighborhood, which is quite enough for conversations, discussions and bickering over who is a cleverer, more resourceful and more agile manager of their virtual team.

Where was I? Before the whole story of the advantages of gaming and small and big children's education; of the positive influence of sport events and small talk on human development; of keeping the brain occupied for the sake of physiological and mental health; of the importance of the liquid vitamin B intake, ah, yes, I really wanted to go to the café for some small talk and a pint.

Identification

As I was saying, it is important to be temperate. A pint has a beneficial effect on my body. It works its magic. It improves digestion, cleanses the urinary system and satiates the thirst. And yes, the vitamin B complex helps me sleep better. But the question is why not a large pint, or even better, two pints? The answer is simple: everything more than a small pint would be counterproductive. A craft version would be a real thing, investing wisely in a quality product, just like with time. Investing in yourself, that's important. I definitely wouldn't pass as a beer person.

The Premier League transfer period is almost over. What do you think of it? Who got a good reinforcement? I have the feeling that everybody managed to do a good job except for my Liverpool. We bought just one good player and sold three. There are so many fronts to be won with so few players. How can it be done?

I have always loved it when people identify with the teams they cheer for. We bough. We sold. Who exactly are we? You are just a football fan! A supporter! And except for the pleasure that you get from watching the game and rooting for the team, you have nothing, absolutely nothing to do with the team. They just perform for us, spectators, supporters. There's no we. They are over there and the rest of us are here. Or is it? The answer is two-fold but the fact remains that each supporter identifies with the team they root for and it just shows how much the players' enthusiasm is appreciated and to what extent a supporter recognizes that and identifies with the team. Namely, there are supporters who are born into the whole cheering-for-the-team tradition, and there are those who chose to become one. Some would argue that it has to do with religion, but it is a completely different topic that I don't want to explore right now. Whether you are a supporter by birth or by your own choosing, with sound mind and clear conscience, you identify with your team's successes and failures. You recognize its effort and are ready to praise and reprimand. Just like in business. There is a team of people who work hard, who believe in their product or service and it is obvious that they professionally do their share of workload, which you, as a customer, need to appreciate or depreciate. You identify with a beverage, food item, trade mark because you share the same beliefs. After all, it is a known fact that you don't sell a product or service but an experience that is created around them. That is noticeable everywhere. I remember when the team I cheer for was in financial debt and was brought on the verge of solvency. The whole club is up to their ears in debt. The previous management embezzled millions and the supporters created a fundraiser to help the club pay its debts. Everyone was supposed to give as much as they could or were willing to. Even though we were badly off, we managed to donate. It was not a rational but an emotional decision. We loved the team. Madly. For everything it had given us. For its tradition, the players' effort and enthusiasm, everything. Can such love last forever? Of course, it can. It's an emotional bond, by birth or choosing. That's love. Can that love become hate one day? Rarely, hardly… such a twist is almost impossible. Is the situation the same in the product and service market? No. The market is rough. You have a good product. You have invested years in creating the brand name. You make a mistake. The market, you customers will tell you to fix it or they'll stop buying it. And it is a one-time mistake. Otherwise, you won't get the second chance.

There is no I in the Team

nd a small pint is coming. As is the NBA playoff. I think that it has never been more uncertain. Frankly, I'm really satisfied with the magic I have seen on the court these days. It reminds me of Michael Jordan at the end of the XX century. Everything is about an individual. Back then it was Jordan, who dominated the court. After his era, the Black Mamba era ensued, picking up where Air Jordan left off.

Now, hold on a second. The most notable individuals who marked the end of the XX century and the beginning of the XXI were Jordan and Kobe, but as far as I know basketball IS a team sport. The wizards such as Jordan and Kobe were always at the center of the game, literally as shooting guards or small forwards, and metaphorically speaking, since they did their magic and won games, but what were all the other players on the court doing? Playing background roles? I don't think so. It is a known fact that when Tex Winter said to Jordan: 'There is no I in team' and when Jordan responded 'But there is I in win'. This is perfectly true but the game is five against five not one on one. Besides, the most important question is: what kind of *win* do we want to achieve?

One interesting fact is that both players had Phil Jackson as a coach. It is possible that he had his share in the success of the teams. Or did he? It might have been Phil Jackson's hard work and enthusiasm in finding new approaches to basketball that enabled the two to dominate the NBA for so long and so intensely. I'm not questioning their individual qualities nor their talent, hard work and sacrifice. They were the ultimate athletes. I can only bow to them. When Jordan stopped playing it actively, I lost my interest in the game. I'm not saying this as a supporter but as a manager.

I would argue that it was the triangular attack system invented by Tex Winter and successfully implemented by Phil Jackson that was the key to the success of the Chicago Bulls and then LA Lakers. While Doug Collins was the Bulls coach, his charisma and dedication to work and to the team inspired the players led by Jordan to victories. His attack tactic was for the other players to find Jordan and then leave it to him to do what he considered and knew best. To Score and win. They won the games but not the Championships/Cups. It was not how they became the NBA Champions.

Doug Collins was replaced by his assistant Phil Jackson and everything that Collins had stubbornly refused to implement, his successor did. One of those newly implemented tactics was the triangular system of attack. The aim of this tactic was to empower the team so that anyone would be in a position to score. If the whole team was stronger, the chances were that they would be more efficient. The chances were that they would become new NBA champions. Did Jordan like it? Of course not. Such strong individuals cannot accept the fact that they don't control the ball, that they don't control the game. There was a strong resistance to this tactic. However, the secret to a true genius lies in the fact that they need to adapt. When Jordan understood the advantages of the offensive triangle and grasped the gist of the system and accepted the fact that he was the most important but just one of the players in the team, and that the team as a whole could become the champion, the change happened and the rest is history. He was no longer Michael Jordan, the all-time MVP, he became Michael Jordan six-time NBA champion title holder.

Another example is in Europe, Lionel Messi, one of the greatest football players ever. Guardiola enabled Barcelona to play for Messi and Messi to play for Barcelona. With Messi as a part of the team, Barcelona was unstoppable. After the change of the coach, Messi was still a football wonder but without so many titles.

An individual's contribution to the team can be substantial or insubstantial. Hence the MVP award. Hence the stats. And the analytics. Is it a coincidence or a rule? But the team wins the prize. The trophy belongs to the team. Individual success in a collective sport is one ingredient of the overall success but if there is an individual and there is no team, then the war is soon lost.

The battlefield, that is the market, regulates success or failure on its own. Sometimes love wins, but reason is almost always on the throne. We can love the club and the team but we can't love a product or service (actually, we can but it is a completely different kind of love), regardless of the perfect marketing and its perseverance in persuading us to love them. All individuals, as genius as they might be, need to play for their team and if they don't understand the basic principles of their role, that they are a part of the whole, they need to brace themselves for the bitter taste of defeat brought on to them by their own stubbornness.

Oh, how I love professional sport and loyalty to the team! It is a mighty machinery that reminds us on a daily basis what the key elements of success are. Sometimes we can't see the forest for the trees.

The Goal Philosophy Begin

Is this too much philosophy around such a simple fun activity as sport is? It is all taken too seriously, when in reality the game is quite simple. It is fun. Tell that to any supporter of any team or club! What you'll get is a priceless epilogue. Sport is not just that; it is a lucrative business with a lot of money involved. Aren't sport arenas just a substitute for gladiator arenas? Spot is a passion. It is love. It is business, too. However, it is also an act of heroism and chivalry.

Is there any psychology in sport? Of course, there is. Provoking the opponent, which I personally find unacceptable, is a part of sport folklore. Rarely can you see it done with a style. Philosophy in sport usually means doing yoga, meditating or turning to Zen Buddhism. Now this is a lot of philosophy on my part and I've only started the first beer. A while ago I was talking about Phil Jackson, whose father was a priest, and who introduced Zen Buddhism to Chicago Bulls training sessions.

Speaking of philosophizing, have you ever heard of Bob Ladouceur? Don't waste your time trying to find it in your memory bank. I think that even saying that he was a coach of De La Salle High Spartans in Concord, California since 1979 wouldn't help. If you are European, the chances of you knowing anything about Mr. Ladouceur are slim, but if you are American, then you know well who I'm writing about. What makes Bob Ladouceur so significant? His team (we are talking about American football, high school league) managed to win 12 consecutive championships, from 1992 to 2004, which means 151 amazing victories.

Americans are all about stats and results, and that was an uninterrupted long line of victories. For me, something else was more intriguing in that success. How did he do it? Not for the success achieved per se, but for the time his team spent on the top. How did he manage to keep the players focused for so long at a level so high? How did he manage to motivate those players bearing in mind the fact that new ones were constantly coming and the old ones leaving since it was the high school league? How?

I've been reading about it, watching documentaries, doing some research into it and have always gathered the same information. You need to know your team, you need to earn the trust of your players, to understand the game… standard things, nothing particular about that, something that more or less successfully all the coaches do. At one point I found out that all the players would have a meeting before the game, in which they would stand up before everyone and read something written on a piece of paper. It was an obligatory routine that Bob introduced.

Each player needed to write down their game and team-related goals, in the line of 'I'm going to run this much, I'm going to achieve this number of throws…'

The first time I saw a player reading before everyone else what he had written down, it thought that I had already seen it before. With the second player reading, I recognized the doctrine. The training session goal – physical readiness: to do ten additional squats after the session every day. The training session goal – technique: to catch each ball. The game goal: to manage to catch each ball and push to 200 yards in a game, and after catching the ball push, on average, 15 yards more. And each player did so. Out loud. Before everyone.

Goals need to be precisely set, if possible, specific. They also need to be **me**asurable and meaningful to an individual who sets them. They also need to be **a**chievable. Needless to say, they must be **realistic**. Finally, they need to have **t**ime limits set. To end, or for the aforementioned players, to begin with, what was important to write down was the reason why that goal mattered so much.

And wow! The S.M.A.R.T. methodology of goal setting. One of the most fruitful and widely-spread methodologies in business. The key to this methodology, however, is not just in the goals that we need to process through the S.M.A.R.T. matrix but in their being written down and spoken out loud. The key is to create an obligation for ourselves and before others. It has to be in front of us all the time. In that way we create a reminder which will prompt us every day to act upon it and eventually achieve it. That is the most important thing, writing the goals down and saying them out loud.

We can't forget the fact that those players were high school students. Young boys were an excellent shaping material. They could easily absorb and accept new ideas. Some would argue that Bob could impress his viewpoints on them because of his authority but what is forgotten is that at that particular age teenagers are against any kind of authority. I might come back to that topic later on. So, the core of this approach is the foundation rock of almost all world religions and philosophies.

Each individual's success in achieving their personal goals will be something that the whole team will benefit from. The biggest contribution to society comes from an individual who does what they best can do. This is a paraphrase of what Adam Smith, the founding father of modern economy, once said.

Stay in Your Own Lane

What about individual sports or the ones which don't require man's physical strength, such as Formula 1, for example? It appears that all the sports come down to the same thing. How can that be? On the one hand, we have team sports and on the other hand just one individual. Well, just as behind every successful man stands an even more successful woman, in individual sports it is not a successful woman but a team. An individual sports person has a whole team of people who are responsible for the individual's success or failure.

Choose any tennis player. Novak Djokovic, for instance. I've chosen him on purpose, since his rebelliousness and both the spectators' and tennis magnates' animosity that follows him make his success even more impressive. He has a fitness coach, a strategist, at one point he even had a data analyst who had the task to go through all the relevant stats. He has a whole team of people behind his success. He had a nutritionist, even that spiritual guide who helped him meditate and find his focus in the game. They have all had their share in his becoming the GOAT.

It all comes down to team work even in individual sports. I feel deep admiration for one more sport even though I still haven't managed to understand the logic behind it. I might not be so open-minded a person, so intelligent to understand that all the team members take part in the success of an individual. That's fascinating!

Another example is Formula 1. We see individual drivers behind whom there is an army of people whose job is to maintain the racing car. Not to mention the fact that each team has two drivers, and that there is a parallel constructor competition, and to top it all, it is a customary thing for a driver to let another team driver win in the general standings.

A Formula 1 driver is never alone. He has an ongoing radio communication with the team strategist, the team chief, the wisest of them all. In addition to the driver's skills, what brings success in F1 are strategy and timing. Recently, with all the technological advancements and a wide range of accessible knowledge and information, everything is within an easy reach. Almost all the teams have unlimited resources, incredible constructors and mechanics. Almost everything has been invented and available to everyone. All the drivers are amazing, the best in the world. Nuances determine the winner. The key to success is most often the tactic and the race strategy. That's the reason why the wisest strategists, the team chiefs, the leaders give instructions from the box and in that way help their drivers to win or achieve the highest result possible. It has always been like that.

However, an extraordinary thing happened during the Formula 1 race in Barcelona in 2020. The Mercedes-Benz drivers were superior to all the others that year. Their omnipotence was so conspicuous that the first driver had an advantage over the fourth one by a full lap. Some argued that there was no point in watching such races since you could tell who the winner would be right from the start. The reason why such races are worth watching lies in the fact that it is not always the fastest racing car that wins the race. As I have already explained, a large number of trivial things determines the winner. But it is not what I wanted to discuss. Let's go back to the Barcelona race.

Lewis Hamilton and his teammate Valtteri Bottas were absolutely dominant in this race and they came first and second. Somehow, I'm still unsure how Max Verstappen from Red Bull Racing had got between the two of them during the race. The ensuing battle was fought with all their knowledge, power and possibilities. Max Verstappen was in constant communication with his team, his chief, to get his counsel as to what, where and how everything was to be done. He received advice, suggestions and incessant reports on the track conditions as well as on the main opponent, Lewis Hamilton. He could hear the man saying on the radio what Hamilton had done or how fast he had been driving or the sector he had been in or the kind of result that he had scored. Was the situation going to change after the first pit stop? Lewis changed the pneumatics. Max followed suit. Lewis had opted for the slower but not so expendable ones whereas Max had decided on the softer ones that would enable him to be faster but would also be quite expendable. Max would try everything just to catch up on Lewis. With his team on his side, he fought valiantly but Lewis was still faster. Even though Lewis had slower pneumatics, Max couldn't catch up. He received new messages from his own team that Lewis was still faster and that he should somehow try to be faster and that they would keep him informed on both Lewis and Bottas.

By now Max had understood the situation. There was no way that he could gain on Hamilton. Hamilton was faster that particular week, maybe even season; for him, Hamilton was, at that point in time, beyond reach. But he knew that he was much better than Hamilton's teammate, Bottas. If his focus was on Hamilton, whom he couldn't gain on, he would neglect his own race. Focusing on what seemed unattainable, he wouldn't be able to see what was achievable for him. Whether Bottas would gain on him or not was irrelevant. He was not driving his race. Both him and his team were so focused on the opponent that they had all completely forgotten about their own driver, his race and all their responsibilities.

It's ok to know what your opponents are doing but the point is not in the competition. The key to any success is us! We need to focus on ourselves, our race, our obligations. Only then can we be better because the most fearsome opponent that we have to deal with is us again. We are our own ultimate challenge. If we give our maximum, if we stay focused on our fight, if we stay in our lane, we might not win the race but we will learn in the best possible way and use all that knowledge to win in some other races. No matter how fast the Formula 1 racing cars are, it is still a race, not a sprint but a marathon!

Max Verstappen understood the reality of things and sent the following message to his team 'Let's focus on our own race, for a start and forget what Louis is doing. It is obvious that although our pneumatics are softer, we are not as fast as they are. So, let's do our job properly and leave theirs to them.' When you think about it, that was a lot of business wisdom coming from a man who was, at that moment, driving at 300km/h under the 3G force! That's insane!

The secret to success in any undertaking is in work. Effective and efficient work. Working on the right things at the right time. It is also essential to be mentally involved during the process. Mere coming to work and getting things done in a routine fashion will not increase our productivity; nor will it create any additional value. We will not become better. The only way for us to become better at what we do is to contemplate what and how we do it. It is good, necessary even, to see the details of the market and business but the main focus should remain on us and our work. We need to become the essential part of our own business decisions, our own life. If we follow in someone else's footsteps, we will learn something about those people but if we want to learn something about ourselves, we need to thread our own path, look back at our own steps and in that way know ourselves. We need to beat ourselves and the only way to do it is to get to know ourselves, our first opponent, better. This is our toughest battle, for the enemy is full of excuses and mimicry and knows exactly when and where to hide. Such a cunning adversary! We need to chase him down first, corner him, get to know him and then go into the decisive battle.

In the following season, the same person, Max Verstappen, overtook Hamilton in Mercedes in the last lap of the last race and won the champion's title. His being persistent and resolute paid off. I deliberately emphasize this information on Max Verstappen because I was writing about him a year prior to his success. The writing process is still not over but the starting premises were obviously correct.

Are We on the Same Page?

Modern athletes are so arrogant. There's too much money involved so the game slowly loses its charm. Why did somebody have to pay an enormous amount of money for Messi's termination clause before all the conundrum? I do understand that it is all business but they have crossed the line. Sometimes I have the feeling that they believe they are a kind of football deity. They have been building their tower of Babylon for quite some time. At one point I think God will get angry and tear it down. I also think that they don't speak the same language anymore. How many different nations do football players of one team come from? Can they understand each other? What quality can their game be if they can't communicate even some basic things to their teammates?

Let's look at a player that Zidane brought to Real Madrid for quite a lot of money. A professional player who proved himself in the Bundesliga can't even make a pass in the new context. It goes without saying that a player needs some time to adjust himself to a new team and his new teammates, but for this particular player the adjustment period has really been long. Somehow, he cannot find his way around. On one occasion I spotted that particular player by the out line being explained by Zinedine Zidane what he was supposed to do. All the time he was staring blank at him. Is it possible that a player doesn't understand the language his coach is speaking? If that was the case, why couldn't you Mr. professional football player learn a few words of the language that the coach would use to talk to you after all the time spent in the club? And you dare to lay the blame on others for not playing well? They don't pass the ball to you. And you couldn't learn a few words! So much for being a professional athlete! You are doomed since you lack the foundation. Playing football and kicking the ball is not the foundation. It is the coach's strategy and the way you implement it on the football pitch. You could do it if only you understood what you are told. Unbelievable!

A year before Jürgen Klopp became the Liverpool coach, he had started learning English. Guardiola had done the same thing before taking over Manchester City. That's how real professionals do it! Thorough preparation is the key to everything. The foundation. Elementary! How can anyone in the whole wide world do any kind of job without being able to understand the interlocutor? Needless to say, nowadays the knowledge of a few foreign languages is almost mandatory. Elementary school children learn two more foreign languages along with their mother tongue. But let's not talk about education. Let's focus on the use of a language.

When Sir Bobby Robson took over Sporting from Lisbon, he couldn't speak a word of Portuguese. A problem. Luckily, a boy from Portugal could speak English quite well, so as Sir Bobby Robson once said 'I had the feeling that as passionately as I was speaking to my players in English, the interpreter conveyed it to the players.' Therefore, it is not just what is said but also the way it is said. That interpreter followed him to Porto and then moved with him to Barcelona.

The name of the interpreter was José Mourinho. He didn't mind being called the interpreter by Sir Bobby Robson throughout his career although he did tactics and the opponent analysis, which later became Mourinho's trademark. He set his pride aside and started 'stealing' knowledge from Sir Bobby. He wanted to learn how to become a great coach, only to become one of the greatest in the decades to come, surpassing his old master.

Mourinho was not much of a football player but he really loved the game and he was looking for his chance. He got one as an interpreter. Mourinho, an interpreter. It is said that he speaks English quite well. To this day I haven't been convinced of his mastery of the language. What's more, in my humble opinion his English is everything but perfect. And that's the point. You don't have to be perfect. Mourinho was wise. He seized the opportunity which was offered to him and used it well. He wanted to become a successful football coach and was ready to put aside his vanity and pride to achieve his goal, and we have all had the chance to witness how vain he can actually be. Vanity is his middle name! The man who calls himself 'special' cannot but be vain! Knowing all this makes his sacrifice even bigger. He was heading towards a higher goal. His ticket for the hall of football fame was his knowledge of English.

Some would say that he was lucky. I would say that he used the given opportunity well. However, the odds are that he himself created that opportunity. He is a top-notch businessman. A stroke of luck! As accurate as the saying 'Fortune favours the bold' is, I'm more inclined to believe that fortune follows those who work hard and try hard. Fortune favours the persistent and brave.

Every success is grounded on a clear, simple two-way communication. How can anyone understand others if they don't speak the same language? How can anyone be so irresponsible not to invest the last atom of his mental power and learn the language that others use to speak to him and that he himself would use to convey his thoughts and ideas to them as well? You want to be a professional player, and not just any kind, but the one who plays for the most prominent football clubs, then you need to work on yourself. How hard do you try to be favored by fortune?

The Ease of Walking Away

For quite a long time, people have been talking one and the same thing about Mourinho. He is said to drain the whole team out of their energy in three years' time and then walk away when the proverbial ship starts sinking. He has done it with Porto, Chelsea, Inter, Real Madrid and finally his tactic got disclosed with Manchester United. Mourinho, the heir to Sir Alex Ferguson? No chance! There can be only one Sir Alex Ferguson! I have always wondered whether it is more complicated to be a constant manager, a leader of the same team or to change companies, that is, clubs from time to time?

Let's take 'Mr. Special' for an example. He managed to bring Porto to the top of Europe. Porto! That year's absolute outsider! Mourinho knew what he was doing back then. He knew how to bring his team to the top of their physical readiness in two years' time. He used the advantages of both the team and the individuals just as he used the weaknesses of each and every opposing player. Porto played really awfully but the results were outstanding! It is always debatable whether the results are the most important thing or the beauty of the game. As for myself, I always vote for a good game, not the results. What I have liked about football are the beauty of the game, the players' determination and the results have always been second to that. The way I see it, if the players give their best and if the game is good, good results will follow. Even without the trophies, the game is what matters. It has to be good. Whether or not it is the best game of the year is unimportant. It would be nice but is not obligatory.

After Mourinho had left, Porto fell apart. The players were sold for a lot of money and the club became history. We will never know whether Mourinho could have repeated the same success had he remained on the top of the club. He went to Chelsea. The same story there, too. Amazing success and after some weaker results, interestingly enough around the third year of his being there, he left for Inter. Again, a similar situation there. Excellent results, the team won the Champions League, and he left it for Real. History repeated in Real and he went back to England, to Chelsea again, but achieved no results, and then to Manchester United as Ferguson's successor, but the situation there was even worse…

So, what is more complicated: being constantly with one team or achieving success with different teams? Both options are really hard but I think it is somewhat more complex to be a constant with one team, that is, in one team. If you come as a coach to a new team, that very act creates euphoria and a new force for fighting. If you have been with the same team for a long time, you need to introduce novelty to prevent apathy. Mourinho addressed that particular problem by going from one club to another. Let's put this in a different perspective. When things get rough in a marriage, and they definitely will regardless of how perfect that marriage is, you don't flee that union to form another one. You try to save the one that you are in. It is difficult, strenuous, unpopular but it is still your marriage that you will be trying to save. I'm not trying to say that it is something a modern man is running away from, both family and business-wise. However, the truth is that companies are not overjoyed when they read in someone's resume that the candidate has changed a lot of companies. And yet, the opposite is true for the top management. How come?

It is possible that companies are preoccupied with becoming an instant success. They all want top results right here and right now. Is it achievable? Yes, but it comes with a price, and a high price, I might as well add. After a five-minute-glory period there comes the moment when the coach and similar players leave the club, and you as the manager haven't done anything to solve that problem in a systematic way since you have been preoccupied with instant success. There are so many examples of this. But are there any examples to support the opposite claim? Of course, there are. I will just mention one. Bayern München, the shining example of a good organizational structure, wealth preservation and not overpaying the players. Long-lasting devotion to the club. On some occasions they even provided financial help to their direct opponents, one of which was Borussia Dortmund. There are many theories why that happened but I find my own theory most plausible. If Borussia Dortmund is not strong, then Bayern München can't be strong either. Now, that is a real company. Who the manager is, is not of the utmost importance. Even if the manager is not good enough, the system is strong and there might be just a year of bad results, and that's it!

Rarely do you have excellent company management and an excellent coach at the same time. For instance, when two institutions such as Sir Alex Ferguson and Manchester United join forces, success is guaranteed. However, Sir Alex Ferguson wasn't an institution when he came to Old Trafford. He became one along with the club. Manchester United made him the institution, and he repaid it more than he'd ever imagined he would.

Could Ferguson have left after the first few bad results? He could have but he chose not to. Could he have left when the end of his career was drawing near, when he'd already become the greatest of the greatest? Of course, he could have, but he didn't want to because he knew that a difficult transition period for the club that had to go on without him was ahead and there was no one suitable enough to continue where he left off. He wanted to contribute as much as he could while he could. He was not the type of a person to leave when the going got tough. Just as with everything else in life, that job has ups and downs. Ferguson stayed until his retirement; he fought until his last day. He succeeded in what had once been thought unimaginable: he managed to overthrow Liverpool and place Manchester United on the throne of English football. And he didn't achieve that by giving in. He fought valiantly. As for Mourinho, at this point I don't want to speculate about the reasons for his failure at Man United. Personally, I'm not really keen on careerists, but that is something I have to deal with.

The Road to Success

Mourinho might have lacked vision, but Ferguson surely had it. It would be fair to say that the two of them had different visions. Mourinho's was closely linked to his personal success, whereas Ferguson's was linked to the success of the club, which would then result in his own. That is, in my opinion, the biggest difference between the two managers. Mourinho was good only for himself, and Ferguson was good for the company.

If you are an employer, think of a manager that you would like to have in your team. The one who will bring instant success and an even steeper downfall or the one who will try to create a system that will bring about success in the long run. To put it differently, if you take a bank loan, will you spend the money or invest it? Too rough a comparison? How about this: if you take a bank loan and buy a nice car and an amazing apartment, you will be successful with ladies. Those few years might be the best time of your life. By the time that car becomes dated, and your apartment doesn't look that amazing anymore, everything will be back to square one. What's more: it might be even sadder. You need to find the money to pay for the loan, and money is sparse. Everything has been spent. However, if you use the money to invest in the future, build a family house, you will have the opportunity to create a home, and that is something you will benefit from for a long time. Here, the question is not what the correct thing to do is but which option is wiser.

It is one thing to go through a turbulent period of youth on the road to success and a completely different thing to grow mature and become a man. Ferguson's beginnings were tumultuous and filled with success. His unbelievable Aberdeen triumphs recommended him to Manchester United and he, as a real professional, wanted to prove his worth in the new environment. He needed a challenge worthy of his ambition. And he got one in the United. The greatest challenge for him was to take Liverpool off the football throne of England. At that moment Man United had 7 champions' titles and Liverpool 18. Great challenge, wasn't it? So, he got down to business.

The beginnings were difficult. He took over the club in 1986 and won his first title with Man United in 1993. At the end of his career, the score was 20 for Man United and 18 for Liverpool. Not only did he manage to gain on Liverpool, but he also succeeded in beating it and in that way exceeded all the expectations.

Ferguson set his own ambition bar high. He had a long-term plan, which was not about his personal achievements, but was also about the goals of the company he worked for. That's the point of this story. Companies need to recruit people that will consider it their home. In its turn, the company needs to make sure that its employees can feel it as their home. Nowadays, when everything revolves around fast changes, fast business decision making and instant success, that is easily forgotten. The excuse that one cannot strive for a patient and steady growth because that isn't supported by the modern economy is just an excuse. No wisdom in there. Again, it all depends on the employer, what he wishes for his company and how he wants it to be achieved. Finding the right people for achieving that goal is one of the most difficult parts of that jigsaw. You need a lot of wisdom to find them and even then, the fight is not over. What's more, it is then that the fight begins. As an employee, you need to arm yourself with a lot of patience, before everything else. Why? You need to allow some time for your employee to use the opportunity given and do the job he was hired for in the first place. It also involves a lot of selfquestioning about the decisions that you've made as the company owner. Particularly when things don't go as initially planned. Did you make a good choice? Can you see the results? That's the reason why Fergusson is a good example for company owners and managers alike. A company owner needs to have faith in his choice of his managers and have a clear insight when things go downhill. A manager needs to have faith in himself when the going gets tough. There has to be mutual trust. A company is an organism that can achieve success only if it functions as a unit, a team. The foundation of any team lies in mutual trust.

Fergusson didn't come to the United to get affirmation as a coach. He wanted to achieve something greater than that. He wanted to make Man United the best team in England. He had a long-term goal and had the idea how to achieve it. He knew that he was in for really hard work and he accepted the challenge. As he once said, 'In this line of work, you need to make unpopular but right decisions' That is the key to success. That is serious business. You must never give up on your principles and always believe in yourself. Here, persistence is often mistaken for stubbornness. I sometimes say to my children that a persistent person sticks to their beliefs and finds ways to overcome all the obstacles along the path to success, whereas a stubborn person will bang their head against a brick wall trying to get across the obstacles.

Success often makes us falsely wise because we lose the ground beneath our feet on its wings. That's the reason I believe it is more complicated to repeat success than achieve it the first time round. Sir Alex Ferguson's greatness could be seen after Aberdeen won the Cup of Scotland, ten days after it had beaten Real Madrid in the

Cup Winners Cup. While everyone was celebrating the victory, Fergusson said, 'This was embarrassing. We played badly' This statement shows that success per sei is not particularly important. What is more important is the way it was achieved. Again, I always tell my children to learn from both their victories and defeats. Of thy sorrow be not too sad, of thy joy be not too glad. If you work diligently and patiently, success will ensue. It is important to do things right. Success is here, the cup has been won, but not how we agreed to be done. It's unforgivable. It might not be important to the ones who care only about success, but the wise know that victory and defeat are just different sides of the same coin, and the way we get to either of the two shows who we really are.

Living Mechanism

It was easy for Ferguson to achieve success when he had the resources and infrastructure behind him. Isn't that the situation with almost all the big clubs, yet not all of them achieve the success that Ferguson has achieved. Aren't most managers in the world now in a position to achieve the greatest success in their industries, yet only a few actually do so? All the players know their job, but some achieve success and others do not. The essence is not whether someone knows how to play football or do their job, but how they do it. A group of people does not make a team. What are the things that make it?

To begin with, we must have quality players, quality employees, and then help those players and employees do their job to the best of their knowledge and ability. They are aware of this themselves, so why point it out to them? True, but they need to be a team, which is why they need a leader, a manager to lead them into battle, bringing out the best in them. The one who makes them better, to the point where they surpass their own capabilities. Although they do not surpass their capabilities, often they are not fully aware of what they are actually made of, so they need a leader. In addition to a leader, there must also be a team captain, the one who takes care of everything on the field according to the manager's instructions. Everyone has people, but few have a team, a real leader, and a good captain as well.

First, let's see who should be the captain? Should it be the best player on the team, the best employee? No, not at all! Although this is a common belief, it is completely wrong. The best football player does not mean he will be the best captain. He is undoubtedly the best football player, but that does not qualify him to be the best leader, even though this is regularly done. If this regularly happens in companies and teams, it does not mean it is correct. A team leader must be the one with the best leadership qualities, who allows the team to be better, who deals with leading people first and foremost.

Based on this, shouldn't the best coach have been the best player once? That's right. Top coaches were often terrible football players. They couldn't play it well enough, but they could lead teams very successfully. There are so many examples of successful managers in the world, precisely those who were clumsy as players, but who loved football and wanted to prove themselves as coaches and were incredibly successful in doing so.

When the famous coach Arrigo Sacchi was reproached by journalists for his qualifications to be the coach of a club like AC Milan and told him, "How can you be a champion coach when you have never been a champion yourself?" he replied that he didn't know you had to be a horse to train horses. Touché.

It has often happened that coaches who were football players did not succeed in their coaching job because they simply were not leaders. They were excellent players, but they were not excellent coaches. They understood the game, but they could not convey it to the players. Perhaps they were excellent strategists and tacticians, but that knowledge was only for them. Could it be that they had no one to pass it on to? If so, they are poor at selecting players. Bring in players who play not only with their feet but also with their heads. Those who think. Famous Fabio Capello often said that a match was not won with legs but with the head. Not to mention the stars in the teams, their vanity, adapting to a new environment, the way they work. The selection of staff, players, is a very complex and complicated process. You must be up to the task of leading.

On the road to success, there are too many obstacles, and each of them must be overcome. One of the biggest challenges is assembling a good team. Human resources department, can you hear me? First, I need to know what I want to achieve with my team, and then I need to know who I have on the team. If I don't have what I need from the available resources, I must ask for the missing part of the team to be provided, because such a mechanism, like a team, must have all the components in order to work. All the cogs in the machine must be in place. But that's not the end. When you create such a mechanism that works excellently, it must also be properly maintained. It must be allowed to operate smoothly in order to carry out the tasks that have been set before it. If we have all of that, then we can go into battle.

It often happens that some parts of this mechanism do not work properly, and these are often its vital components. They must be repaired urgently. Some can be fixed, while others have to be permanently replaced with new parts. You have to make decisions that are not popular, but are correct. As was the case with the key part of Manchester United's team machine, Roy Keane, who had to be removed from the team because he threatened to ruin the whole machine. Was he a vital part of the machine? Yes. Could his actions have ruined the entire machine? Yes. The decision was difficult, but logical. The long-time captain of the "Red Devils" had to leave the club. Was this an isolated case? No. The same path was taken by Jaap Stam, the heart of United's defense, and Ruud Van Nistelrooy, one of the best forwards in the history of the sport. All these cuts were painful, very painful, but they had to be done. One rotten apple threatened to spoil the whole basket.

No one is bigger than the team, the company. If someone is bigger than the team, then the team will no longer exist. We could attribute this to the laws of nature, logic, or any law. So why do so few people adhere to these laws? Why do we see in practice that players are more often bigger than clubs, rather than clubs being bigger than players? Why are these the rules, and not the exceptions?

The answer is really imposed by the nature of human personality, its weaknesses, vanity on the one hand, and on the other hand, the answer lies in the business that revolves around the sport itself. The desire of sponsors for profit intentionally pushes, that is, encourages the inflating of vanity among the players themselves. A sensation is needed. It is necessary to create a cult of personality that will sell tabloids, jerseys, sports equipment. What benefit does the player get from such self-promotion? Finally, their five minutes of fame have arrived. This is the reward they have worked hard for throughout their childhood. So many years of sacrifice will finally pay off. And it is true. That's really all there is. Those five minutes of fame are indeed just those five minutes of fame, and nothing more. After that, it's all over. You are no longer a team player, your club (company) can no longer count on you because you have mixed up your priorities. The club (company) you play for is the master you serve, not the other way around. Priorities are hard work on and off the field, and with all the accompanying show-business trappings, you can no longer devote yourself to what brought you to that pedestal where everyone crowns you. Those same people who push you into that world will soon, very quickly, condemn and crucify you. It's time for you to continue your journey at another club. Experienced managers know this and try to prevent it. They must prevent it in one way or another. Either they will heal it or amputate it. It is inevitable.

When Chelsea goalkeeper Kepa refused to leave the field because his coach Sarri wanted to replace him, that was the end. The end of the team first and foremost. The outcome could have been either Kepa leaving Chelsea or Sarri doing so. Sarri left the club. In both cases, the team suffered a loss, but in my opinion, the greater loss was Sarri's departure over Kepa's stay.

We have an example of a player like Messi, who, without adequate coaches, leads Barcelona to success with his charisma and skill, but that too was doomed to failure. No matter how hard he tried, attempted, and had the best intentions, he failed because the team is always greater than the individual. The Champions League final ended with Bayern Munich demonstrating, with a "symbolic" score of 8-2, that the team always triumphs over the individual.

A team, as a complex organism, a plant, must be maintained properly and watered daily. You cannot expect your favorite flower to remain the most beautiful and to survive at all if you don't water it daily and maintain it adequately. Why do you think business is any different? Someone would say that there is not enough wisdom in managing a company, or a team. Someone would say that it's all in accordance with nature. Everyone has ups and downs. That's true. That's why wisdom is given to people to prevent falls, to surprise the future, to create it, and not to be surprised by the future and be served what they did not want.

What is, at least to me, not clear enough is that self-promotion is encouraged in some companies. For an employee to stand out from the crowd of workers, it is necessary to work on self-promotion. I'm not saying it shouldn't be done, but often department heads, due to insufficient experience, promote experienced salespeople who can sell themselves excellently as they sell their main product or service, but as a rule, they do so at the expense of the team.

Self-promotion is reflected in adequately performing assigned duties, surpassing goals, coming up with innovative proposals, and increasing productivity that will be recognized by a superior, which is actually his job. They need to independently recognize, see it, and not be pointed out to it by someone else. To make their employees the best. To enable them to be up to their tasks, to help them give the best they have, and not to buy the one who can best sell their work. To return to the sports field. It's like a football player's manager selling his client to you as a coach of a club, and your decision depends on the skill or sales ability of that player's manager. Where are your scouts? Or when renewing a contract with a player who is already in your team, and your decision, instead of depending on the reports of a conditioning, tactical coach, psychologist, and your assessment, is based on the sales skills of his manager. What's the point of self-promotion if one of the job descriptions of a superior is to know the value of their worker and how much they mean to the company they work for? Employee evaluation is a daily job. Everyone must be responsible for their work.

The moment a player threatens to become bigger than the club, it is time for that player to leave the club. The same goes for the manager. In both cases, the player and the manager, they start working for their own benefit, not for the benefit of their club (company). The one at a loss is the company (club) in which they are.

Burnout Syndrome

There are coaches who burn their teams out in a very short period of time. When those exhausted players have nothing more to give, they remain in the club and the coaches move on to continue their careers in some other clubs. This is unbelievable but it's true. They are indisputably excellent tacticians, strategists, analysts; however, they are no good in the long run. It seems that their effort is timed for a year or two and then it declines and they leave the club. This practice is excellent for instant success but, as I've previously mentioned, this particular game, the business in itself, is not a sprint but a marathon. A company needs to outlive its successful managers. It needs to exist long after we are gone. At least this is the way any wise entrepreneur needs to envision it.

It would be like bringing in an amazing sales manager who floods the market with your products to the extent that after his departure from the company, when he leaves as the manager with the best results ever, your long-time clients call you and ask to return the goods that were delivered to them because they can't sell those quantities or the expiration dates have passed. You recorded incredible results with that manager that year, but in doing so, you damaged the trust of your longtime clients. We all know the importance of not only initial but repeat sales. We all know how difficult it is to acquire new clients. And how much more difficult is it to retain existing ones?

Choose wisely, not those who are just eager for success and proving themselves, but those who are eager for knowledge. Choose loyal, hard-working, diligent people who share the same values as your company, your team. Choose them and then nurture and protect them, respect them. All together they must be one big, successful, happy "family." Not only will egocentric, self-sufficient operating endanger your business at an external level, but it will also shake the foundations of your internal structure. Burned-out players, burned-out employees are a common occurrence due to such operations. Burnout syndrome in the making.

Machiavelli said that the end justifies the means, which is increasingly being introduced as a practice in modern business. But the consequences of such a practice are not discussed; in fact, after the burnout syndrome has been mentioned, everyone falls silent. Employees fall silent out of fear, and employers, or bosses, seem to choose not to talk about it because it's best to bury their heads in the sand and pretend it's a fabrication, an excuse for modern man to find justification for his lack of commitment and poor results. If that's the case, why then, as if by unwritten rule, after achieving top results, is there a general lethargy in the continuity of operations? Some would say it's due to being carried away on the wings of already achieved success or due to a lack of motivation for new victories and new challenges, but in essence, it's a classic burnout syndrome. After timing perfect readiness and pushing the team to the limits of endurance in achieving the ultimate goal, there comes emptiness. Those same players can no longer provide even half of what they offered. And what have we gained? We have gained long-term aimlessness resulting from such team management.

The fundamental difference between careerists and those managers who care about their club is that careerists do not run their business domestically. They operate as if nothing will remain after them. And the end result is indeed such. After them, there is desolation. They leave on the wings of glory and leave scorched earth behind them. So how did Ferguson manage to achieve top results year after year for so long without ruining the company? He succeeded by leading his team, his club, valuing and respecting it. He didn't lead it just for his own glory, but the glory of the team. And he ultimately shared in the success and the glory of the team. So similar, yet fundamentally different.

Again, it's the law of nature. A cheetah can run very fast but for a very short time; after that, no matter how much it wants to, it can't even move a paw. A person can give their maximum for a short period, and then they need to rest. Even an engine can operate at a high number of revolutions for a certain time, and then, if it is overdone, a malfunction will occur. Blindness to success at all costs leads to collapse, breakdown, and ruin.

Let's clarify any possible ambiguities right away. This is not about focus and timing the form. Everyone knows that this is necessary and obligatory on the way to the goal. Here, I am talking about the wisdom of achieving top results over and over again. This is about success at all costs. Who needs Pyrrhic victories?

How to respond to such challenges? It is not simple and it is not easy. There is no unique solution. It is crucial that we become aware of such a danger that lurks at every step and in every place, and that, as with any potential challenge or a challenge that is already there, we must deal with it and talk about it. If there is a will, there is also a way to find a solution.

The Best of What You Have

Do you think you will succeed in winning the European champion title for two years in a row with Porto or Red Star? We should not mix the historical achievements of the "small" clubs with the successes of the "big" clubs. The two can simply not be compared, and all fans of the "small" clubs should forgive me. These "small" clubs lack sufficient financial resources, the player and infrastructure potential. The vey success of these clubs immortalized in the title of European champions is magical in itself. A story that will be passed down from generation to generation. That success, those years with those players were magnificent. Happiness! The success they had dreamed of came true. The impossible became possible. Impossible? If they achieved it, it means it was possible. They didn't achieve it just because they had dreamed of that success. They could dream as much as they wanted, but they had to roll up their sleeves and make an effort to turn their dream into reality.

The success of such clubs is precisely an example that the match is won with the head, not the legs. This example proves to us that if each individual, who is part of that team, does exactly what the coach tells him, exactly that, in the way the coach shows him, success will come as an inevitable result. This is where the skill, knowledge, and wisdom of those managers who have won trophies with such clubs lie. And there are plenty of examples.

A team made up of the players, without the possibility of bringing in world-famous reinforcements, presents a *fait accompli* to the manager. This situation itself pushes him to be better, to get more out of his players, to make them the best. A real challenge. And with the development of the team, the players themselves develop along with it, becoming better. This is a cause-and-effect relationship.

The phenomenon of bringing the most expensive and most popular players to big clubs, who later do not contribute even half of the value they were paid for, is always justified by secondary earnings made only on the sales of that player's jerseys. A completely justified and logical marketing move, but for money and fame such players can destroy the whole team. Envy appears among the players. Such big names usually, but not as a rule, bring their ego to the club, which is often bigger than the reputation of the club itself. Discord arises, affecting the team's performance. However, business is business. Clearly, everything is done for money and I understand that, but I can't justify the loss of the future if such players are allowed to "take over" the team and destroy it. The team's manager must recognize this and adequately deal with these dangers. This is one of his roles and, once again, he is tested for authority.

There is no such thing in 'small clubs'. Limited funds limit the emergence of such stars. A lavish life for every player privately is inevitable, but it must also be sanctioned. In "small" clubs, there is no huge money. A little money spoils a person a little, whereas a lot of money does so too much. The old Latin saying about honors changing people's behavior is something that must be taken into account at all times.

A 'small' club coach must fight with what he has, and in such situations, true values and team spirit come to the surface. All the advantages of the team will be used as will all the qualities of individuals and everyone will give their best to make the team better. They will help each other, cover for each other's weaknesses, and encourage each other. They will be a team. If the opponent is superior, they will use their heads while playing even more. You have to be wiser if you can't be physically fitter. You can't be a better technician when, realistically, you're not, nor be better in aerial play if you're shorter, which is why these are real challenges for such clubs. Their games are rarely beautiful to watch. They usually play anti-football but are admirable because they fight as a whole. You can see how the players implement the coach's strategic idea. Everyone knows their place, a pleasure for the strategist, a horror for the fans, but also a horror for the fans of the opposing team. The famous Otto Rehhagel, the coach of the Greek national football team, managed what few others have. He managed to enable the Greeks to win the European Championship in 2004 with anti-football. Oh, how hard it was to watch! He killed all the beauty, all the charm of that wonderful game, but he was a favorite for those who loved tactics. The Greeks defended themselves throughout the match and carefully and patiently waited for that one attack from which they would score the winning goal. And they succeeded! They really did. Unbelievable. Hats off to the team.

Loyalty

Astronomical transfers serve nothing but themselves. There is nothing there but money. In the past, players moved to new clubs hoping to make a name for themselves, to quench their thirst for trophies, to be remembered as the most famous footballers in history. Now it's mostly about money. Rare are those who do it for the right values.

We must not forget those who remain loyal to their clubs (companies) from the beginning to the end of their professional careers. Ryan Giggs, Steven Gerrard, Francesco Totti, Paolo Maldini, and others did not stay in their home clubs because other clubs did not want them, or because others did not send them offers, or because they were afraid of changes, but because they found what they were looking for in their home clubs. Those were their homes. I am not saying that we can always find top players in our ranks and that we can always create them from our youth squads, but I am saying, and emphasizing, that we must always work on this and always strive for it because by doing so, we invest in our future, in the future of our team, that is, our company.

I do not want to consider remuneration which differs from industry to industry or from position to position within the same company. I want to see why the salaries of newcomers are sometimes higher than those who have been in the company for a long time. Why transfers of players from other clubs exceed the earnings of those players who are loyal to the club. Mistake? Yes. Many people realize this and work on correcting it, but I am still fascinated by the attitude that the grass is always greener in someone else's yard and that something foreign is much better and of higher quality than what we have in our own home. That is why it is easier to buy what you do not know well enough because you see it only through the results, which can often be disastrous. On the one hand you pay and overpay for that player because a magician is coming, at least on paper, and on the other hand, you diminish the importance of all your current players. Here, your new colleague has managed to negotiate a better salary, and that means he is better than you. But what about those who are loyal to the club (company), who have spent their entire working life there and shed their blood, sweat and tears on the field for that club? You must honor them with respect, especially at this moment when the market dictates such a crazy pace of the game of changing club jerseys. It has now become so frequent that the market has begun to mock those who do not change their clubs. They are considered not good enough. Loyalty awards used to be given to those individuals who were devoted to that one company, but now, even if you wanted to give that award, you would not have anyone to give it to. Few are those who have stayed in one company for more than ten years. They exist, it's not that they don't, but they are rare.

Respect those who are loyal to you, and if they are good players, respect them even more. Do not take their loyalty for granted. They may have stayed because they did not have a better place to go, but more often, they have stayed because they are happy where they are. Do not take this lightly, and do not force them with your negligence to seek happiness elsewhere. If they are good and significant, it is of exceptional importance to tell those players, to point it out to them, to let them see that you recognize their work, commitment, and loyalty. To show them how much you appreciate them.

There is always a fear that the staff we are building will leave us the moment they receive a better offer. And they will, when they get a better offer, not when they get a higher salary. The right people do not leave companies just in search of more money but of better conditions. For those who leave because of money, sell them at a high price and wish them all the best, like everyone else, but with the desire that they never return to you, and those who leave for better offers will make you wonder where you have gone wrong. Could you have provided them with a better offer? What could you have done better to retain such staff? On the other hand, if you have already done everything within your known and unknown power, and the player has still decided to seek happiness elsewhere, wish them the best of luck in their future work.

Focus on the Team

We have a club that has enough resources to bring most of the best players in the world to their team. Will that ensure their success? No chance. Will it bring them closer to achieving it? On paper, absolutely yes, but in practice, it hasn't really turned out that way, because there are still a large number of factors that affect success, and it's not just about bringing the most expensive and best players, but making a team out of those people, which is actually the essence and an art in itself.

So, we have financial resources and bring in the best from the labor market. And, what are we doing? We go, watch, search, study players, and prepare money to pay for them. Success guaranteed? Not at all. All serious entrepreneurs know that nothing is certain. It's a business risk, an investment in an uncertain future, but that's how it works and must be done. And if the investment fails, then what? Next time, start over again, but wiser, and yet no less uncertain. I'm sorry, but there are no guarantees for success.

But, let me get back to what I wanted to say. We have a player on the team who gives his all. His good performances have caught the attention of the competition. The competition is getting closer. It doesn't matter whether he has a contract clause for an early departure from the club or not, the competition is ready to pay for it. What happens? "Small" clubs do not have the financial resources to keep him in the club, or more precisely, they live off such transfers, but let's shift the focus to "big" clubs. They have the financial resources to keep such a player, but they often make a crucial mistake, they do not want to give a corresponding financial counteroffer to the player. The player might not even leave the club because he likes it there, that's where he started, his teammates suit him, the coach is fine, everything is as it should be, and his wife likes the city they currently live in, but an offer comes that cannot be refused. More precisely, the question is whether such an offer will be repeated. What does he do? He accepts the offer and so the unraveling begins. The club loses a key player they could have kept, but they didn't provide an adequate counteroffer. We will find, create another one, or even more common practice, we will buy another one, is the logic many clubs follow. The success rate of buying an adequate replacement is very low. How much time does it take for a new player to adapt to a new environment, new teammates, and the coach's new philosophy? But that's the job, we move on. Let's see if we could have kept him? We could have given an adequate financial counteroffer or we could have built such a relationship with the player that he wouldn't even think about the financial structure of the competition. We need a good HR strategy as a basis, and then a myriad of things that we had to do much, much, I emphasize, much earlier. Why is this often not understood? This is the foundation of every company, every team. The team is composed of people, they are the basis of everything. You can't easily replace such a player. What, we lack business experience? Come on. This is the way modern business functions? Yes, but that means we're floating instead of swimming. What did we do to prevent this? Well, that's the art, the strategy. Serious work that nobody wants to do because it's difficult, demanding, complicated, exhausting. You have to dedicate yourself to the player, you have to focus on the team. You only think about the results and how you will easily find a replacement for such a player in the market, because everyone plays football today, because everyone is a professional today. Well, that's the difference between a good and a great club. Principles and practices are what will make that club huge, and that is so hard to create, hard to achieve, and can collapse like a house of cards in three seconds. Puff and it's over. After that, it's very difficult to return to the old paths; it's possible, of course, but the road is very arduous, and we could have prevented it all.

Now let's look at all these events from the player's perspective. A change of environment is being offered to me. Great. Every change is good, fruitful. Such an offer cannot be missed. But everything in my club is as it should be, why should I change? Wait a minute, why didn't my club offer me something like that? Don't they value me enough? I know they can pay me. And off we go! The decision is made by itself. It's too late to stay. The next question arises, why is it most often the case that players' incomes increase rapidly when they move from club to club? Why can't incomes within the mother club, which can financially afford it, increase so rapidly? Why is it most profitable for me to seek happiness in someone else's yard rather than in my own? Because very often the management is blind and deaf to the player, the individual, and the essence is that such management has a detrimental effect on the team and the club they lead. There is no domestic business, and I'm not talking about revenues and expenses here, but about the vision of the future that must be woven from the past and the present. You can't sleep on the laurels of history. Of course, the pillar of defense for such attitudes will always be the need for fresh "blood" in the club; this is an inevitable process of prosperity, a common thing in today's business. To me, it looks more like an excuse and justification for poor work, and least of all like domestic business. We've had ups and downs in form, motivation, results, of course, this is normal. This is the everyday life of modern business, but you can't say that the new girl in your life will take away all the problems that were present with the previous one. That second one will leave too, you'll "sell" her as well. You'll replace her with someone younger and better. Come on. You can do that with a toy you've got bored with, but this is business, life. Come on, come to your senses a little! Struggle a bit to be wiser, it will do you and others around you good.

Empathy

When you have great potentials in your teams, try to employ them in an adequate way. You must provide them with opportunities and ensure conditions for unhindered development. Give them a chance to shine. Now, this is a double challenge. One lies in recognizing these tendencies in your employees, and the other is being able to facilitate the process of their development. Recognizing talent alone is a detective's job. Some are readily available, others don't even know what talent they possess, the third are persistent but without talent, and so on endlessly. The important thing is whether they are coachable. Say goodbye immediately to those who are lazy and those who are full of themselves. Both you and they will waste time and energy there. Everyone must be ready for a constant change, adaptation, and learning. They must be prepared to work hard on themselves. How will you recognize them? It's not too difficult. In fact, the largest part of the job is observing, listening to them, and talking with them. Taking care of them. Don't assume, assumption is the mother of all screwups. Conclude, don't guess. The truth can be different from case to case, and you must find theirs. You must see things from their perspective in order to help them and guide them. By helping them, you will also help yourself. It is necessary to allow them the right to make mistakes. Everyone makes mistakes. Build them a safe harbor. This doesn't mean that you won't hold them accountable in their work, that you won't question their poor performance. On the contrary. You will only focus on why it has happened. You will look for the cause, not the culprit. You will seek ways to help them be better. That is your task. By serving them, you serve yourself. This means that you won't put them on a pillar of shame when they make a mistake; there will be no guillotine, no shooting. If you look for a solution, you will find one. And yes, it is demanding and exhausting. Nobody ever said it wasn't. That's why you are a real manager, up to the task. That's why you are where you are, because you have the knowledge and can take responsibility and do the right thing when everyone else loses their head.

You must first find the truth through conversation. You must communicate well with the players. Start by communicating. And now you might think I'm kidding. You're mistaken. All the things that are crystal clear to all of us, all the things that are right in front of our eyes, can be often perceived differently. Do you remember that viral internet story about whether you see a white-gold or black-blue dress? It's impossible not to remember. Well, if you don't remember, here's a brief refresher. One and the same picture, and people see different colors. Of course, I thought it was some kind of joke. For me it was white-gold. So obvious. I know colors, right? I thought, what a stupid thing, the stupid things that could be found these days on the internet. I showed it to my family, and they also saw white-gold. Everyone? Nope. My son saw it as black-blue?! How? Well, he did. I told him to stop messing with me. And he was not. He wanted to know why I assumed that he would be messing with. I didn't tell them why I was asking, I just asked what color the dress was. I was in shock. I did some research on the internet and found out that this phenomenon even had a name. "Color constancy." Mild disbelief. I peeked into Pandora's box and said, let's see what else was in it. And then another shock ensued. An audio recording. Do you hear "Laurel" or "Yanny"? I heard "Laurel," my wife heard the same, but the kids heard "Yanny"?! How come? I was frozen with fear. Everything became questionable. I could no longer be sure if what I saw and heard was the same as what the other party saw and heard. A few minutes of fear, and I made a decision. The truth is what I believe in, but that doesn't mean what the other party says isn't true, even though it's different from my truth. Long live the differences! We just have to agree on the truth we will follow on our path to success. There's no point in following someone else's happiness when I want to find my own.

Understand your players. Make agreements. Bring your truth closer to them. Lead them. Provide support, understanding, and comfort. Communicate. Observe them. Encourage them to open up, be honest, and tell you what is bothering or annoying them. Remove obstacles in their way. Teach them how to remove those obstacles themselves later on. Give them the strength to show their vulnerable side, but show them yours too. You are in the same boat, eating the same bread, breathing the same air. Be there for them. Help them. Give them strength. Believe me, it's mutually beneficial. You have to give something to get something in return, and is there a better feeling than helping others while helping yourself? Priceless.

Journey

You are now watching a player who is trying their hardest. They are dedicated, hardworking, and absolutely doing everything right in the training session, but for some reason, their contribution on the field is simply not yielding results. The team is not achieving as expected. Once again, I emphasize that the individual is part of the team. The individual works for the team and contributes to the result. But there are no results. It is possible that the coach has set a bad game strategy, not to mention the fact that other players must also give their maximum in accordance with their abilities, and that team, and with it that player, is still not achieving the desired results. Results simply do not exist, and this starts to affect the player's self-confidence, as well as the confidence of the team, and the impression is that the player is not good enough.

The conclusion is obvious. For someone to show their maximum and their true qualifications, many factors must be in place. It is necessary to have a good strategist, a good coach, a good team captain on the field, and to play with people who share the same values and the same desire to succeed. It is crucial that they have the same work ethic and approach to tasks on the field as well as the work ethic in the training sessions.

You are trying really hard in the training sessions, giving more than you are asked to, eager for success, exposing yourself to so much effort that there is a real possibility of injury and a danger of ruining your career. Why does this seem to me like the story of "burnout" at work, after which, if visible results don't come in a normal period, a person burns out in the desire for success?

And then what? Does that mean you should give up? Does that mean you shouldn't even embark on that journey? No, not at all! The point is not the destination. Good work ethics, effort, and dedication will enable you to know yourself first, what you are made of, what obstacles you are willing to overcome; how much you are willing to sacrifice, endure pain for an uncertain future. To know what makes you human. You never know where that journey will take you. How can you know? You can only wish and visualize the goal, and no one can tell you what will be achieved. The goal may completely change, but what will be a constant in its realization is you.

The current coaches' dedication to their playing careers has made them what they are top-notch experts who don't give up, who play until the last minute, cheer on their players, inspire others with their charisma, and who don't give up when things go downhill, when the game doesn't unfold according to the scenarios they envisioned before the start of it, who adapt to new situations on the field. That's what needs to be conveyed to the team. Will it bring success at that moment? Maybe yes, maybe not, but that way of thinking, that way of working needs to be rooted in the team, and it will start giving its maximum at every moment. It is the mindset that matters, not the result. This will give you an answer to how to approach both success and failure. While one can learn from success, the wise can learn even more from failure. The essence is in dedication.

In the end, all that hard work and dedication will make that player, coach, anyone, the person they are today. They will draw from their previous experience and use it in their daily battles. Isn't that the process of learning? Of course, it is. It's painful, arduous, and uncertain. And now what? Should we give up? Only those who don't want to be better, who don't understand the essence, give up. Charlie Munger often said that the foundation of failure was giving up quickly. Who said everything would be easy and fast?

It's like writing a book. The biggest obstacle is the blank white page in front of you. You look at it, it stares back at you. You start scribbling something, you see it's not working, but you don't give up, and after some time the words start to flow on their own. Absolutely. The result doesn't come from nothing, but from your previous efforts. How many times have you started something new or something similar, but in a new environment, in a new team? First comes fear and disbelief, new environment, new people; then comes the feeling that you're not making progress, and then comes the most unpleasant feeling of all, regression. Then comes questioning. What am I doing? Is it my fault? That's when it's important not to give up, because these are all phases that absolutely everyone goes through. After that comes progress. At last.

I had the privilege of working for some of the world's largest companies and having some unforgettable experiences through the regular activities accompanying those jobs. We were testing some new vehicles on the track in Barcelona, where a professional rally driver from Australia taught us to drive in rally conditions using the latest vehicles from our range. He told us that when we go very fast through a passage, we should always focus on it, not on the cones. If we focus on the cones, we will hit them. The moral is, if you focus on the solution, you will find the solution, if you focus on the problem, you will find the problem. At that moment, I had a picture in my head of a driving student practicing on a rural football field, moving from one side of the field to the other. He drives slowly and heads towards the goal, and you think he won't hit the goalpost on such an empty field, but he does. His focus was on the obstacle, not on the passage.

It's all about talent... as if. Talent is something desirable, but it is not what guarantees success. Success is 3% talent and 97% hard work. We can discuss the percentages, but that's not the point of this story. Life is work, practice, effort, a difficult struggle for every bit of knowledge that you gain through it. That will make you the best. The best for yourself first, and that way you will be the best for others. You are a part of a team. If you are good to yourself, you will be good to others. And we come back to what I've been blabbering about all this time. If you do something, if you try and give it your all, but only think about the result, not the process itself, if you don't understand it, if you can't see the whole picture, then the matter is lost. You must give meaning to everything you do. You must be aware of every moment, every effort, but you must not think only of the goal, of victory. The journey itself is the point, not in the destination.

Moderation

Players have all sorts of things in their contracts. There are bonuses for attackers based on how many goals they score or assists they make, and for goalkeepers based on whether they concede goals or not. There are all sorts of things to be seen, but I came to the part that says how many times they appeared in matches. Wait, they get a bonus for showing up for work?! Either we are crazy or they have gone mad. You motivate an employee to come to work not with restrictive measures, but by rewarding them for having played a certain number of matches. However, I do think they are right. Positive stimulation is always better than punitive measures. Employees are more committed, take better care of their health, and try not to get injured during the training sessions and outside. Will this maybe have a negative impact on their performance on the field? There is always a possibility of that, but it will be immediately apparent and a good manager will react accordingly.

Will this logic of treating employees come to modern companies? Honestly, in those companies with wise management, it definitely will. There aren't many of them, but they exist. There will always be those who say that the worker will abuse such treatment. Of course, they will, of course, there are such cases, but should we give up being wiser and creating something that is realistically good for our job just because there is a possibility of abuse? Of course, we should not give up, of course, it will be difficult, but it will be good for our players and our employees and our team and our company.

Isn't the path to progress connected with the threshold of pain? You will never be able to stretch your tendons and increase your body's flexibility if you don't push your body to its limits, that is inevitable. This is the only correct way to progress, but you must be careful not to overdo it, as the limit is thin and self-injury can easily occur. What does the company or the team need at that moment, the best individual or a functional team? A functional team always wins. What's the use of injured players who pushed themselves so hard in the training sessions that they jeopardized their health and thus endangered the team? Look, it's like that story about overworking yourself at work. You burn yourself out at work until you burn out. Who needs someone like that afterward? No one, absolutely no one. You do too many things at work, work ten or eleven hours instead of eight, and forget that there is something else besides work. What are the consequences, will you become smarter? You will, but you must not overdo it because you will jeopardize your basic functionality. No matter how much you practice your shots on goal, a third leg will not grow out. You will undoubtedly become better, but if you overdo it, there is a real possibility that you will overburden your muscles and become completely dysfunctional. Who benefits from your excessive efforts then? Nobody, not you, not the club, not the company. What to do? Should you strive and expose your body to pain to improve performance? Yes, of course, but like everything in life, it should be done in moderation. Moderation must exist in everything, both in life and in business. Take care of yourself for your own sake, but also take care of yourself for the sake of the company. There will always be a multitude of well-wishers around you who will know what best for you is. Trust me, you know much better than anyone else what is good for you. You know your body and your mind best. Only you can determine your pain thresholds that you can endure without compromising your functionality. Don't forget that you are the only judge. Conditioning trainers can help you, but they can't know better than you what you need the most. Managers are the ones who must know when and how to time the team's and individual's performance. They must direct. That's what good leaders do. They know when to tighten and when to relax. They have to see, monitor, what, when, how much, and how. That's their job. Under the condition that they know how to do it and are willing to do it properly, of course.

Active Listening

You provide the player, the employee, with everything. You enable them to work under absolutely impeccable conditions, give them the opportunity to improve themselves, and create an atmosphere that is phenomenal for work, and yet they leave, they leave the club (company). Yes, they leave, it's a business risk. It's in the job description. You try your best, give it your all, but there's always the potential for the employee to leave and go their own way. Realistically, it happens, even more often than usual for some. And now what? You need to be honest with yourself first and see if everything, absolutely everything, was done properly on your end? Did you do everything to make sure the player could find their happiness within your team? I'm not talking about any fluff or superabundance, but about whether you were actively listening to what your employee was saying. Every time you ask a manager, an owner, if everything was done properly, they will all say that they did everything they could; and yet their employees still left the company.

I have just remembered that conversation between the CEO and CFO. When the CFO expresses their concern about investing in people who may leave the company tomorrow, while the CEO expresses their concern about what to do if they don't invest in people and they stay.

A friend of mine has an extremely serious approach to business. A healthy, versatile approach. The man has always been a few years ahead of his time; he has created not one, not two, but five companies that operate successfully albeit independently of each other at the same time. He is a phenomenal and successful entrepreneur. He says, 'I have a problem with employees nowadays. I give them the opportunity to learn and gradually ease into the job. I provide them with mentoring, a decent onboarding period, all the necessary conditions for a good start and successful development, and after six months, they come to me and say that what they are doing is not challenging enough, that they would like stronger projects where they can contribute more and feel better. He says, "Great, I'll give you what you wanted. I'll give you everything you asked for. I'll even give you time and space to think about it, come up with the best approach to tackle the problem, and prepare yourselves for new challenges. The epilogue of this should be a ready, hardworking player, eager to get on the field, show themselves to others, and compete. But it doesn't work out that way. The common epilogue is that the worker resigns. How can they resign when I did everything they wanted? I provided everything, we agreed on everything, and they still left. Tell me, how does that happen?' I sit and think about it. I start from the fact that this is a common case in today's business world. You can invest and not get a return; trust people and be betrayed. That's all fine. It happens, and it will keep on happening. But one fact still haunts me. Did you really listen to what your employee was telling and showing you, or did you only hear what you wanted to hear? Something is suspicious, and that suspicion permeates through all similar situations I've encountered. Everyone is convinced that they hear and see the same thing, but it's essentially a personal experience, personal perception, which is highly subjective and affects our assessment. The same thing happens when we communicate something, thinking that we have done a perfect job in presenting something we wanted, but in reality, we didn't pay attention to our diction, body language, or the tone of our voice when delivering that information. This now leads us to another aspect of information transfer to players, colleagues. Has it been conveyed effectively? Have they been adapted to the listener? Have we paid enough attention to gestures when delivering this information? Why do we think it's only important to present to clients and potential investors? It's necessary to recognize the importance of information transfer to our colleagues, both in everyday meetings and when strategizing the company's movement and future trends. Not to mention that the presentation doesn't only last those five minutes of the pitch; it's a comprehensive, continuous process that follows us every day. We're always observed by subordinates, superiors, children, friends, basically everyone we come in contact with. Whether it's Sauron's eye or the eye of the most caring person, the essence is that we're always under someone's watchful eye. Someone is constantly measuring us. We mustn't forget that beauty and meaning are in the eye of the beholder and only in the eye of the beholder. We're aware of all of this. So why do we think it's unnecessary for us to observe ourselves and others, too, with vigilant attention? How much clearer everything will be for us if we carefully observe both verbal and nonverbal communication, but no, we usually make the mistake of just listening because we want to give an answer and not to understand what is being said to us. And as long as we keep doing that, we will continue to fail. We will always be deceived and caught off guard. How? Why? Well, my dear, just as it is necessary to present well, it is also necessary to listen to the interlocutors in order to be able to perceive all aspects of communication well.

Imagine a coach who doesn't know how to emit the energy necessary for turning things around when his team is losing at halftime. Imagine a player who doesn't understand what the coach is conveying to them and on top of that, cannot or will not express their opinion or concern, or just say "I don't understand." The key to success is good, open, and honest communication, but it's not all the speaker's responsibility; it's also the listener's, too. It's demanding. Yes, it's an exchange of energy that can sometimes be completely crazy and unwanted, but if you want success, if you want to move forward, these are the foundations of the house you are building.

Bad Transfer

There are numerous cases of failed player transfers; failed in every sense. The reasons can be objective and subjective. We can influence some, but not all of them. What needs to be done for the likelihood of bad transfers to be minimized? Firstly, scouting needs to be done well. This process should not consist only of positive, but also negative indicators. It's like choosing a life partner. We shouldn't just focus on the infatuation phase, but we need to think at least one step ahead. Nobody is perfect. Nobody is phenomenal. Everyone has their virtues and their flaws, so they need to be viewed comprehensively. But there is one condition above all conditions. They must be coachable. If they are not ready to receive new knowledge, write them off immediately, no matter how good they are. It doesn't matter how experienced they are and how much they can contribute, you don't need such people. Everyone must be coachable regardless of their experience and regardless of where they are on the team's hierarchy. They must always be ready to embrace new knowledge and be able to develop new skills. They must be able to adapt to any new situation. This is a condition that cannot be waived.

Don't hire people solely on their skills. Of course, they need to possess them. The more and better skills they have, the better, but the key to choosing good players or employees is their attitude towards the job they do. Hire them based on their attitude.

Let's take Gareth Bale as an example, a Tottenham and a Real Madrid player who decided to "misuse" his position in the club and spend his time on the bench of one of the world's biggest football clubs. Why? Because he could get away with it. Because he decided to "repay" Real for the way they had treated him. Was he rude in this case or just true to himself? Whichever the reason for his behavior was, it was not okay. He was disrespectful to the club, his colleagues, and he made bad use of his position. Extremely disgraceful. Was all of that in line with the contract? Yes. Do you want to bring such people into your company? Do you want to do something like that? You certainly don't. Is it possible for this to happen? Yes, indeed. Unfortunately, there is always someone who will abuse their position. Did the employee come with such an attitude, or did he acquire it after a certain amount of time spent in the club (company)? I am sure that this action was not premeditated. It happened as a result of his existence in the club. Well, this shows you that your behavior, actions, inactions, and poor communication can lead your employees to such situations. So be careful. Is Gareth Bale an isolated case? No. We have examples of Sánchez, Özil, and Aubameyang. I am writing this now and concluding that a large number of these footballers exhibited such behavior while playing for Arsenal?! Are these players themselves like that, or is the environment in which these players work and live the main cause of their attitudes? There is a lot in this equation. Everyone has their share in and contribution to this process. Nothing is one-sided and uniform. All of this is the result of many factors and influences, and we must always be aware of them all.

Once you have brought in a long-awaited player, an employee, in your club (company), having searched high and low, everyone is happy, full of enthusiasm. You have finally found a solution to your problem and the action is about to start happening. You paid an abnormal sum for that player. You are sure that he is worth every penny. Maybe you're not, but the market dictated the price. Supply and demand are what conditioned your business decision, and that's it! You saw a potential solution and said, "I have the means to finance it," and consciously paid that price, and now the implementation of that valuable asset has begun to solve business challenges. Okay, it takes time for the player/employee to adapt to new situations. You are ready for his onboarding period, and it's not always great, but now the investment will start to pay off. However, there are no results. The investment is not yielding the desired results. You've blown the money and got something you didn't ask for. It is outrageous! You wonder what went wrong? Who made the mistake? Well, there can be many reasons. Potential headhunters did not do their due diligence for this employee. But you also looked at him and had an interview with that person. You were blinded by your desire to solve the burning issue, and you did not realistically evaluate the potential solution. Now there is also another possibility. It's not you, it's the employee. He simply didn't adapt well enough to the new environment. Maybe he burned out from the desire to prove himself? Maybe he simply has personal problems that affect his performances? Oh yes, that can be one of the main obstacles, whether you like it or not. Need an example? Harry Maguire himself. None other than the most expensive defensive player of the present. The captain of Manchester United. As a Manchester United fan, I write this with a bitter taste in the mouth. The backbone of the defensive line that came to solve all the problems, but alas! He became an additional problem, not a solution. Is he the only example? I don't even want to list them. There are as many as you want. So, what did you see when you hired them? Ok. There is always a margin of error, it's all fine, but mistakes as big as those are simply unforgivable, especially for such corporate giants. Unacceptable. Is that a business risk? Yes. Could the level of risk have been minimized? It could have been. Why was it not? Because someone did not do their job properly. Or was it blind trust in associates that they would choose the best the cause of all that? That could have also been the possibility, but then you need to rethink your choice of associates. Another fire to put out? I would rather say that people do not conscientiously do their job or they simply apply the same logic in business when choosing seniors and juniors. Well, my dear, it doesn't work like that. The same tools and approaches won't always yield satisfactory results. It needs to be done a bit better, with more dedication and understanding.

They say the definition of insanity is trying to get different results with the same behavior and actions. Well, it just won't work. You will have to try harder, to engage more. To dedicate yourself to your job in a more adequate way. Salary must be earned, and it is not earned merely by the time spent in the workplace, but by conscientious and dedicated work.

Negative Selection

Is it possible that there is so much amateurism present in the professional world? What's going on here? Things used to be quite different: that if you were not good enough, you couldn't play with the best. You could only sit next to the sideline and watch the game. Now the situation has drastically changed. Is it due to a lack of quality staff, or is the influence of self-promotion so strong that it's starting to take its toll? Or have managers and headhunting agencies started to do their job sloppily, pushing half-finished products as finished solutions? Anything is possible. There are many factors that influence all of this. Take, for example, a headhunting agency that offers what it currently has on the market due to a lack of quality workforce. Their job depends on it. They don't think about their reputation when they are faced with the possibility that they will not exist in a few months. You can't live off reputation. Let's face it, if they do a shoddy job, they won't last long, but will survive. Perhaps capital protects itself. It's possible that bad business decisions are justified by the state of the market. This is what's on the market and this is our reality. Despite the fact that we all know it's not good enough, we try to sell it at the highest possible price, and if it's gone, it's gone. We'll push our merchandise. And where's the condition for a job well done? Who cares about that anymore? If the worker I sold turns out to be no good, I can always blame the company for not being good enough to embrace such staff and provide them with the conditions for fast and unimpeded work and development. And so on and so forth. Responsibility no longer exists; it has disappeared into the thin air and become nothing more but a memory.

And what of the player's responsibility? That employee whose performance was deemed poor? The cunning ones will always seek excuses and justifications.

Those who aren't will lie low and keep quiet. They won't stick their heads out in this unscrupulous market because they have an excuse that it's impossible to find their place in the sun among a plethora of hotshots and self-promoting individuals. Excuses abound, but results are missing. Finally, poor selection has begun to yield results. They say that it's enough for good people to do nothing for evil to prevail. Well, it's true. Burying our heads in the sand and not calling things by their real names has led us to this situation. It all started when we began to call problems challenges. The essence isn't in that, but rather that a problem is a problem and a challenge is a challenge. It's becoming increasingly common that when we call small problems challenges, they eventually turn into big problems.

And good people still do nothing and stay at home, trying to stay out of the way of these rude, self-serving individuals. These semi-humans, self-proclaimed professionals, have even begun to promote their way of life and their doctrine of laziness and non-commitment as the key to success. They promote deception as intelligence, explain the ways to cheat in an exam, and avoid the burden of responsibility. So, who's the crazy one here? Oh, right. For that matrix to succeed, they need to surround themselves with similar people, thereby giving legitimacy to their actions. Some private educational institutions have produced so many poorly qualified individuals and keep on pushing them into the economy and the marketplace to give legitimacy to their way of life. Chaos isn't emerging but is already here engulfing us. There are no more real journalists, real politicians, real players, real workers. It's an excuse after excuse. Will their poor performance be seen? Yes, but the machinery is so fast that they won't be remembered for long. Time inevitably passes, and someone has to pay for their mistakes. The company, the club, the taxpayers will pay. Now, those are what we call problems, my dear, not challenges.

Think

The referees in today's matches are a story of their own. Yes, now there are a myriad of sports competitions and a large number of sports, and it is impossible to achieve everything, but that is not an excuse for chaos. Let's face it, lower-level leagues have always been able to withstand such blows of incompetence, but that's what those lower-level leagues were for; for profiling real referees so that they could deserve to officiate big games. And now, instead of having experienced referees, we have a group of semi-professionals who should not even be allowed to officiate children's games, yet they officiate the most important duels of today. It is understandable to make a mistake once, since everyone has the right to make a mistake, even to make a mistake twice, but with all these technologies, with all the id and the cameras that follow every moment of the game and after all the testimonies of their bad decisions, they still officiate the most important sports events. I won't name them; you have such examples every day on all TV channels. Everything has gone to hell.

Now I remember those TV broadcasts of sports events where it was known who the directors and who the cameramen were. Yes, in the previous century there were not so many TV broadcasts and the best people were chosen for those jobs. Everyone knew what they were supposed to do. They were real professionals. Now the ball is on one side and the camera is on the other. The director drinks coffee instead of managing the broadcast. What the hell is happening here?

Again, the negative selection outcome, or maybe something else here at play? It's all about chaos and negative selection, and those who don't do their job well always come up with excuses that they are overburdened with work and that the world has changed. If the world has changed, why haven't they adapted? If they are overburdened, why don't their superiors manage better? Why haven't they been taught how to conscientiously do their job? Instead of striving for better and more professional performance of their duties, we get an insufficient quality product with excuses for the things that could have been done better. There are too many excuses. So how can we achieve better with such an attitude? Realistically, everyone has the right to make mistakes, that is perfectly natural and normal. But do we learn from those mistakes? It seems to me that we don't.

While thinking about this, I'm immediately reminded of a few exemplary cases from my hometown which boasted exceptionally tasteful pastry in the previous century. I'm not talking about the pastries made in privately-owned bakeries, where they fought for quality and for the customer, but in the state-owned, or rather the social sector. That social sector is a story in itself. Anyway, I've been through all kinds of systems in my life, communist, liberal-democratic, democratic, and a few dictatorships, a few wars ... and so on.

But let's get back to the pastries. It's true that everyone's childhood is painted with beautiful colors, and even if it wasn't that great, we always remember it as beautiful. And in my childhood, there were a few wonderful places where you could eat pastry for breakfast. We didn't go often, but every visit was unforgettable. We had privately-owned bakeries and state/social ones. Well, one of those privately-owned bakeries made its own yogurt and cheese-filled rolls only. The man was narrowly specialized and did his job exceptionally well. Interestingly, it seems that the importance of specialization for achieving success has somehow been forgotten; instead, companies focus on diversifying their products and services. Until recently, I believed that true entrepreneurs were completely aware of this and fostered this philosophy of doing business. However, I realized that most of them blindly pursue expanding their product range and do not understand the basis of their business and existence. I would say that the absence of basic knowledge of economics is at play here. It is as if someone has erased thirty years of economics and condemned those who knew something about it to forget or suppress that knowledge so deeply that they never remember it again. The key is in specialization. Look at so many of the world's most successful examples: Amazon, Google, Apple. They did not start with a wide range of products but rather with narrowly specialized business models. Only after they had grown enough to embark on expensive business ventures and excursions, where they could endure the pain of entrepreneurship, did they venture into the unknown. And knowledge is now accessible to everyone. Once, a wonderful man said that we must be careful who we learnt from because bad teachers could lead us astray. Mark Twain said that we needed to read a lot, but we needed to choose the right books. It seems that the curse of choice is at play here, but in the end, we will become Buridan's ass. It is so obvious. How can they not see it? Well, life moves fast, there is no time for thinking. Come on, who justifies not thinking? There is only strictly inert action. Who gives the right not to think, not to include reason in the decision-making process?

I always give my children the same example on this topic. We all have a need for the toilet. Let's not go further to find a more appropriate example. Everyone has to go to the toilet. You know you have to go to the toilet and you start heading there and there's no need to engage your brain, right? Well, you should. If you don't engage your brain, you'll make a mess. You have to engage your brain to take off your pants. Now, people confuse this with routine actions like taking off your underwear when going to the toilet and don't think about it. Well, my dear, that's practice. You've done it so many times that you've forgotten that you're doing it now automatically, intuitively, without thinking. But think, always think. That's why you need to practice constantly, several times a day, the same operations to become a perfect shitter. And today's generations think, because everything is at their fingertips, that a flash memory is enough, which they just plug into their brain and immediately learn. There are no shortcuts to success. None! Overnight success is the product of 15 years of hard work. So don't confuse intuition with infinite repetition of certain activities until they have become routine. And don't forget that even when you become a master shitter, you still have to practice. Why? Because some pants have a clasp, some have buttons, some have zippers. Not every challenge of going to the toilet is the same. It also depends on the stool consistency, response speed, distance to the target. You have to practice constantly because there are no two identical pieces of crap. You have to practice so that the challenge called poop doesn't become a problem.

Anyway, let me get back to what I was writing earlier. And how did we get from food to poop? Well, because those are two sides of the same coin.

Let's go back now to those state/social bakeries that my country used to be proud of. Mind you, if we exclude the lack of product quality control, as well as the quality control of raw materials from which these products are made, (there is no point in controlling the economy so strictly, they have to turn a blind eye somewhere. But let's start with the assumption that the quality of the ingredients is the same now as it was thirty years ago, which it isn't, just as cars aren't the same as they were thirty years ago, neither are croissants, but let's say they are the same.) then how on earth is that damn croissant not of the same quality now as it was at the end of the last century? It's not even close to what it used to be. And I wouldn't be me if I didn't complain about it at the source. I found a man who made them, to explain it to me. 'I have a problem, you see. Try to understand me. I can't buy a normal pastry or croissant anymore. I'll go crazy.' And I asked him what the problem was? What's going on here? He laughed and said there weren't as good raw materials as there used to be. Everything was being cut down on. The global economic crisis has hit our small town too, but he said there was something even more significant, even more terrible than that. He said all those who had known how to make them right, all those old masters, had retired and when they had left, they hadn't passed on their knowledge to anyone. I asked if it was for the lack of their will or the lack of time, and he said both. They didn't want to because their employer thanked them nicely for their forty years of work in the company and sent them into early retirement because they were expensive, old, unprofitable, so they decided to keep quiet and take revenge in that way. And there's the other thing. Some of them wanted to pass on their knowledge, but they had no one to pass it on to, because no one wanted to do that job anymore, it was too difficult and poorly paid, and those who were there were not able to absorb the knowledge that was being transmitted to them. And then the employer decided to make the proverbial lemonade of what he had. Of course, the ultimate price was paid by the dissatisfied customer. Now, if you're a monopolist, you don't care about the consequences of your business, but if you're not, the market ruthlessly punishes such behavior and neglect towards quality, and it will 'reward' you nicely.

And now, let's go back to cameramen, judges, players, and employees in companies. Why do they do their job so sloppily? Are they not capable of absorbing new knowledge or is there no one to transmit that knowledge to them, so we have returned to the Stone Age in the era of the greatest technological achievements and digital transformation? We have computers, but we don't know how to read and write, which in itself raises the question of management responsibility. Do your seniors transfer knowledge to juniors? If they do, do they do it adequately? Do they do followups? Do they follow the development of younger generations? These are all questions that need to be answered. This is a process that a manager must follow. That's your main job. The future of the company depends on it. Or is it all about profit? Instant success? Give it now, give it right away, because who knows what tomorrow will bring! There is no width in thinking among those who are not dedicated and not educated enough, who work in a haphazard way. One time wonder. Is that the point? This is sustainable development. A continuous path to success. A constant struggle with challenges and problems that makes us stronger and stronger every day. You've confused things a little. The 'successful' masses have blinded you. Well, those successful people have been imposed on you as well. And you, what are you doing? Waiting for something to happen. How can something different happen if you're not doing anything about it? On its own? Do you want to call the elevator without pressing the button for its arrival? How do some people imagine that? And there are those who say 'I pressed the button, the elevator came, but it didn't take me where I wanted to go'. Of course, the story doesn't end with calling and getting in the elevator. When you enter that elevator, there are buttons again. You have to do something again. It's an infinite game that requires actions, reactions, interactions. You always have to think, always work, always fight, always hope.

Dirty Dancing

How many people don't want to get involved in their own lives under the pretext that they have tried everything, that they don't want to waste their time and energy on the people and surroundings that make them miserable? And everyone is completely aware of the problematic situation that we are in nowadays and they all say that they have tried everything but nothing could be done against the charlatans around and that their final reaction is that they quit. Never wrestle with a pig; you'll both get dirty and the pig likes it. That's all fine. Choose your battles but go for a win otherwise the half-breeds will prevail. They have started to indoctrinate our children with their philosophy. I can't explain to my own children that if they cheat on others, they actually cheat on themselves. That it is absolutely irrelevant whether people notice and recognize your work and efforts; they carry all the value. What we need is a mirror to face our own reflection. Self-awareness. And yet, we are surrounded by examples that refute everything that children have been taught by their parents, so they start to question their beliefs and their teaching.

Somebody needs to get down to business. The business which is never finished by the pretenders but by those who are silent, hard-working and tolerant. Those who have the mirror. People should bring back embarrassment and shame into their rightful place within the society; only in that way can people be ashamed of their bad behavior, accept responsibility for their bad work and stop with the excuses. Bring back shame and embarrassment into public life! It has become a common belief that cheating on people is to be upheld instead of scorned upon. Bring back shame and embarrassment into schools! What kind of schooling are we talking about? During the two tears of Covid pandemic my children didn't have proper education. Teachers were the ones who played truant, they didn't want to do their job. It was all about the form and not the content. Children were not taught. Naturally, there were exceptions to this unfortunate rule. And from there, children realized that there might be alternative ways to achieve success. But there aren't. Some steps can be skipped but sooner or later they need to go back and revise and relearn what they missed. Everyone is trying to cut the road to success short, which is an expected but not the healthiest way. They are surrounded by bad examples of apparent but short-lived success based on the thesis that life is too short and that we don't have enough time to question our actions, and that we need to make it on our own.

There is a plethora of quasi experts, careerists, everywhere in the world. They are just pawns; no real leaders, only followers. Well, congratulations to all those in power! You have finally succeeded in creating a society of puppets. But what are the consequences of such a doctrine? An army of zombie workers who deliver semi-products. Such a doctrine is good for those in power hungry for money, whereas it is a majority of people who pay for their bills. The smart and educated don't want to partake in building a society of real values when they realize who's involved in that undertaking. People need to be incited to focus on the real values, since it is the only way to sustainable development. The current situation is just a road to the abyss. Aristotle's wisdom that only by touching the rock bottom can you get out of the whirlpool cannot be applied in this context. We are not allowed to touch the bottom. We are in a shithole of lies, in latent stress. There is no up; you just need to swim and be careful not to drown. The greatest trick that the devil ever pulled was convincing the world he didn't exist.

Cause and Effect

Knowledge transfer is crucial in every aspect. On the one hand it is necessary to have those who are capable of performing this knowledge transfer, which implies their ability and willingness to do so, while on the other hand it is necessary to have those who are ready, willing and able to embrace, accept and adopt this knowledge.

Neither of these sides was born with such abilities, so it is necessary, as is with everything else, to first study them well, and then learn and eventually master them. It is also necessary to teach the student how to acquire and internalize this knowledge. Do you think people are born with these skills? They are born with predispositions, and skills need to be developed, worked on, and practiced. They need improving. Even when these skills have been mastered, it doesn't end there. It is a continuous process that never stops. Habits, methodologies, approaches change, both in the market and in the mental framework of teachers and students. Learning and skill acquisition models evolve constantly, on a monthly basis. It is necessary to adapt to trends, to be in line with all the aspects of the market.

I love consultants who come and tell us what needs to be done in the company by presenting the same methodologies in the same way. They come, tell their story, take the money and say, 'That's it from us, now it's up to you to implement this.' 'Wait a minute, that's not exactly how it works. I mean, you've told your story, earned your daily wage fair and square, but the problems remain because what has been told needs to be implemented properly and appropriately."

I am not referring to the issue with consultants, which is a story in itself, but rather pointing out that their work should be a process. It goes on indefinitely. It is necessary to constantly monitor students and teachers, primarily through their mutual feedback. Self-evaluation, self-improvement, and recording strengths and weaknesses in every aspect, in every place, and at every moment are necessary. The company is a living organism that must be maintained and cared for. Yes, there is room for mistakes, to err is human, but if we know what our goal is, then on that winding road to success, full of ups and downs, we can disregard mistakes because it is necessary for the goal.

This all incredibly reminds me of going to the doctor. Something is wrong with someone, so they go to the doctor. The doctor listens to the patient, takes a medical history, prescribes a treatment, and then schedules a follow-up appointment. The patient needs to take action in accordance with the doctor's instructions to address the problem, which requires constant monitoring of the patient's health by both the patient and the doctor. Everyone needs to do their part. What happens in practice? Doctors only treat the symptoms while, in the best-case scenario, the cause is only identified. The patient's responsibility for their health is a completely normal thing. To be honest, after the symptom is resolved, the patient often continues to repeat the same behavior pattern that led them to the symptom, so after a certain period, the symptom reappears. And, the patient goes back to the doctor, and the doctor treats the symptom, and so on in a circle. The problem is not solved systematically. The doctor shrugs and says, "It's not me, it's you because you've disregarded the measures that would solve the problem." The patient says, "Doctor, why don't you solve the problem?" And so on, indefinitely.

Every expression in this equation must do its part, dedicatedly and conscientiously, to achieve the appropriate and satisfactory result. Permanent work on problem-solving is unquestionable. It is a must, my dear, a must. Without being reminded of your regular duties. Don't forget that reminding yourself is also part of the job. Someone gets 'lost' on their way. That's why leadership is needed, not mentoring for experienced professionals. It's necessary for someone to guide you, to help you understand what is and what is not essential. It's necessary for someone to lead you, externally and internally. Externally, your managers, your coaches, and internally, yourself. You must constantly remind yourself of your responsibilities and set priorities.

You need someone to explain to you how to win the game, to motivate you, to explain the strategy, tactics, to lead you to success. Additionally, it's necessary to be able to listen to your coach, to implement their ideas on the field, to encourage yourself and your teammates, to score goals, to play both offense and defense. To represent the club (company) honorably, both on and off the field. To take care of the club's (company's) good reputation. To respect yourself, your colleagues, your managers, and the club you represent. Yes, always and in every moment. You have to live your life every moment.

Focus

Identification of potential challenges and problems cannot happen without the adequate implementation of activities that are necessary for an adequate response. We have agreed on strategy and tactics, and now they need field implementation. The fight can begin. Whatever the coach had to say, he can only rely on the captain to orchestrate the implementation of the agreed plan on the field and to trust in the dedication of his players. According to an unwritten rule, what is agreed is never applied absolutely, which is sometimes good because individual contributions and dedication can lead to even better results than expected. Sometimes individual qualities are crucial in the decisive moments of the game because they make a difference in our favor. However, if they are not put in the service of the team and are not aligned with the company's goals, failure is inevitable.

There is a story from the local football club Radnički from Niš. It is a story about the famous Stevan Ostojić (everyone has claimed this story for themselves, someone tied it to Ostojić, someone to Trajković, but nobody should be offended, for the sake of writing a book, let me attribute it to Ostojić) an incredible scorer who is associated with an urban legend from the stands, when he dribbled past one, then another player in the opposing penalty area, then the goalkeeper, and instead of scoring, he returned and dribbled past the goalkeeper again. The coach, unable to watch it all, covered his eyes and asked his assistant: "Did he score already?" to which the assistant replied, 'He's still dribbling him'. It remains an interesting urban anecdote, and we can use this old example to show how someone cannot work in line with the goal set but instead fuddles and fails to realize the coach's ideas. The aim is to score a goal and beat the opponent. It's nice to have fun at work, to have a playful game, to enjoy what you do, but the primary goal must be respected; otherwise, we have done everything in vain. All the tactics and strategies are useless if we do not work in line with the aim. Let us not confuse devotion to the game with whether the goal has been achieved or not. Simply put, it just did not happen, even though we did everything possible to achieve it. This is not such an example. Here, the employee does not have a focus on the goal but on the beauty of the game, on entertainment. And everything falls apart, even though you have all the necessary elements for success. Individual qualities are useless, phenomenal teamwork is useless, if one of the screws of this collective construct is not doing their job in line with the goals set.

Until the Last Whistle

If we go just a little south of Niš, we arrive in the city of Leskovac, which has a football club called 'Dubočica' that once had famous Svetozar Zare Trajković in its ranks, who never gave up and was able to turn defeat into victory in the last few minutes of the game. So, another legendary story and saying were born: 'You never know, Zare is playing'. Yes, that's like the saying 'It's not over until the referee blows the final whistle'. We've had so many examples in football history where the game was played until the referee's last whistle. How many times have the German national team players, through their dedication and mental strength, turned the game around in the last moments? As the famous Gary Lineker would say, 'Football is a game with 11 players on each team, and in the end, the Germans always win'. We must not ignore the mental makeup of the participants in this life game. It's not the most talented who wins, but the most dedicated. Patience, faith in success, and consistency are the keys to success. Now, we have players who, due to a poor development of events on the field, will give up on the agreed-upon strategy and start improvising, which in most cases is doomed to failure. Let's be honest, there are also those who will completely turn the course of the match in their favor through personal effort, but there are also those who will, due to the atmosphere in the stands, instantly forget even their own name, let alone the coach's words before the match. Fortunately, we have halftime when the situation can be summarized. This is an opportunity to eliminate shortcomings and doubts and to agree on a new beginning, a slight change. And of course, there are those moments when everything goes according to plan, so we just need to validate our previous actions so as not to relax and to bring the game to the desired end.

It is necessary to give feedback to every employee when they are doing their job well, with the same enthusiasm as when we criticize them for poor task execution. It is often assumed that nothing needs to be done when things are going well and that there is no need to explain anything further, and that is a trap we often fall into. It is always necessary to analyze both good and bad. Good, in order to nurture and encourage good job performance, and when things are not so good, it is necessary to point out the shortcomings and give directions to get us back on track as soon as possible. It is important to both praise and criticize equally. The only thing I asked of my children was that when they cry, they cry their eyes out, and when they laugh, they laugh their heart out, but they always have to know why they are doing it. If they cry, they must recognize the reasons for their tears and take care to prevent such situations in the future, and when they laugh, they should nurture that feeling and recognize the reasons for their state as often as possible.

You should never give up. Actually, you should if you are absolutely aware of why you are doing it. Often, in those moments, we look for justifications. Don't let that deceive you. The line between persistence and quitting is thin but it exists. How to recognize it? First, be honest with yourself. Find out what you're made of and try not to take the easy way out often in life, because that will deceive you into thinking that you are much stronger than you really are. That tricky trap of subjective self-assessment is common. 'If it's not the way I imagined it, then it's no good'. Well, it's not exactly like that. That illusion is a result of self-love. The countless occasions that it has happened to me...quite often, actually. And what, not to you? It's too difficult. Well, is that what I was educated for? But the point is not in what doesn't kill us makes us stronger. Now forget about Zarathustra. The question is what you are made of. Will you try to run away from every difficulty? You can run as much as you want to, but in the end, you'll be back to square one. You'll be forced to face yourself again. There's no running away or hiding from that. You can run away from it your whole life. Many people do it successfully. But at the end of the day, it's only up to you to choose what kind of life you want to live!

Be like Zare. Zare always gave his all, even when situations seemed hopeless. When his team was losing by a large margin, he managed to score a few goals. Zare always fought. He fought for himself, for the emblem on his chest. And in the end, regardless of the result, he was fulfilled because he had done everything in his power to achieve success. If you don't win today, you'll win tomorrow, the day after tomorrow, or some other day when the scoreboard is in your favor. But if you beat yourself every day, then you'll be the winner every day. The goal is to know that you've given your all for success. Then you'll sleep peacefully with a heart full of satisfaction.

Surprice Factor

They say that the hardest players to play against are those who play with their heads. Not that they use their heads to shoot, but that they think about what, when, and how to do things on the field. Of course, there is also the other school of thought that says the toughest opponents are those who have no idea how to play football. When you try to outsmart them on the field, you can never get that textbook reaction from them, because they, too, being confused, don't know what to do and often end up sticking to you, colliding with you, or, God forbid, injuring themselves or you. You start to dribble and, of course, expect a few standard reactions to that dribble, which you've usually got from anyone you've played with so far, and this one doesn't move. 'Silence on the field'. No reaction at all, you feel like asking him, 'Hey man, have you ever played this game in your life?'

That's why it's always tricky to play against left-footed players or box against left-handed opponents because you're simply not used to those attacks and defenses. Your brain has prepared you for a well-practiced combination, reaction, move, and then, surprise. The left fist flashes straight into your jaw. You did expect that blow, but you weren't really prepared for it. How? Simply put, your habits have prepared you for it to come from a different angle, in a different way. You were ready, but as I said, life is full of surprises, and this one has hit you so hard that it stuck to your face, and you went back to your previous life to discover the reasons why you were punished. I'll go back to the exercise and constant repetition that didn't bring about the desired result, so you started to doubt every step you took, all the effort you put in. But the beauty is in the details. Those details give you an edge. This teaches you that there is no rehearsed scenario for which you will always be prepared. There will always be a surprise factor. Everyday life also shows you that it is important to never let your guard down, always expect the unexpected, but also that the learning process is infinite. Isn't that the beauty of it? How boring life would be without all of that! But it's all tiring, exhausting, naturally, but that's life. Live it as best you can.

I remember a game that we played recreationally as a sparring team with some guys who were preparing for a competition. They practiced their moves on us. People practiced. You always have to follow your teammate who is attacking on the other end of the field in case he wants to pass the ball to you or he misses so you can lay the ball into the goal and so on. Now, my team consisted of the guys who had played football for a long time, but not on the same team. We just gathered together and played with whoever was there. I, of course, played wherever I was needed, as a defender, midfielder, or striker, not because I was born to play all positions, but it was just the way it turned out to be. So, there was no specialization. That's how I went about it, but that's not the point right now. I ended up guarding one of the opposing players, and we had all known each other since we were the same generation, but that guy was something of a sportsman, more importantly, some kind of a wunderkind. He knew everything, was crazy good at some math competitions in school. A truly exceptional guy. Given that I never really watched TV, thanks to circumstances and not wisdom that I shouldn't watch it, I found out later, of course, only when the whole country had already been aware of it for a long time, that my friend had won or had been the finalist of some popular knowledge quiz in our country, and that it was broadcast on national television. I said, this guy was unbelievable. And it was my task to guard him, and he had practiced moves and every time he received the ball, he used that practiced move so well that I naturally fell for it and was fooled at least three times. At one point I said to myself 'Enough is enough!' Now, when he got the ball, I would go to the same side, you had outsmarted me enough; at the same time, he expected me to move in the usual way. I had it all thought through for the next attack. And the man received the ball and started the same dribble as several times before, and according to plan, I went where he wouldn't expect me to go. But I made a mistake. In a split second, I did something I hadn't done before. I got too close to him and made physical contact that gave away which way I was going. And the clever opponent recognized it and made a fool of me again. He implemented his knowledge and wisdom on the field. Learning on the spot. Applying every aspect of what he had learned in achieving his goal. Bravo. But I wasn't discouraged, I also started learning from what was happening. It became a battle of wits. It's wonderful, really, to play with a clever opponent. Then football is no longer football, but becomes chess. The next attack they had didn't go as smoothly. I read their intentions. The balance of power on the field was equalized, at least for a short period of time. We all started to become aware of our opponents and began to adapt our game to them. It was getting harder and harder to create a chance. We started to become a respectable opponent. They learned, we learned, right there on the field, in real time. Of course, they won hands down. But that's not the point of this story now.

Everything is Visible

There have always been footballers who have perfected their dribbling skills to the point where you, as their opponent, knew what they were going to do, were prepared, and yet they still managed to cross you as if you weren't even there in front of them. You watch them and expect and know what they will do, and they do it all and still succeed. Practice makes perfect. They have brought their strongest weapon to an unparalleled, unbeatable level. In those days, before video recorders, you only had the opportunity to meet someone live on the field or watch them, but you couldn't do it constantly, only when the chance arose. Usually someone would tell you, scouts would watch to convey their experiences as accurately as possible. Mission impossible. Then came the era of private cameras and video recorders, and coaches began to watch game footage, study opponents' tactics, analyze the implementation of their ideas on the field. They watched their own games, their own players. Scouts watched video recordings of their potential reinforcements. Everything started to become easier. However, I remember one addition to Crvena Zvezda (Red Star Belgrade) who came from South America. The man just couldn't find his place in Crvena Zvezda. He was neither the first nor the last to have such a fate, and then the joke started circulating that when he had sent his footage on the basis of which the scouts chose him, it wasn't a video but an audio recording. In any case, video recordings have turned the situation in favor of visual analysts because they have long dominated statistical data analysis, especially in sports in the US, and later around the world.

And then we got mobile phones and cameras in every corner. We all had them. You could follow whoever you wanted to. The statistics database spread worldwide and collected and recorded data not only about the match and its course but also about each player individually: the way they shot in which situation, how they behave with and without the ball, how they play with their head, how many times, and a million other parameters. Now, this may be too much information for the average person, but not for analysts and decision-makers who need to know who and when to buy. Some even consider this insufficient data to make the right decision. And of course, we go back to the visual. I need to see it for myself what sensitivity that particular player carries, what attitude he has in the game, what he's like when he wins, what he's like when he loses, the way he treats his teammates on and off the field. What is his relationship with the opponent? Is he energetic or fiery? What kind of goals does he score? Without this information, I don't make my judgment, and this data cannot be found in statistics. For such data, I have to stretch my legs and hit the road. I have to see it with my own eyes. Now everything is available, both statistically and visually. And now it's really hard to hide your secret moves from your opponent, now you really have to know how to play smart. Think about every move you make. Everyone watches you on video recordings, everyone studies you. Try to surprise your opponent with the move that you have perfected and practiced for years. Everyone already knows it, particularly the conscientious ones who have been preparing for the duel with you. You sit, watch your opponent, see how he moves, what he does when he receives the ball, what he does when the ball is not with him. Now everything is visible, there are no more surprises, no more unknowns. Nowadays, engaging in sports has become most challenging since you are completely exposed to your opponent. You have to get used to the new reality. To think more and to continuously improve, evolve. The beauty is that now you finally have no excuse not to work on yourself.

Productivity

Will practice make you perfect? Definitely. But, will you be better if you do everything mechanically and without thinking about the process? Absolutely not. Work and practice without reasoning can only make you good, but if you don't engage your brain, you won't be great. Being the best in every moment in every way shouldn't be a burden you carry with you, but rather a goal. You don't need incredible achievements to validate your willingness and desire to move in the right direction. You need dedicated work that involves thinking about the process itself.

If you lift weights without thinking about the technique, you can easily injure yourself. If you want to increase your muscle mass or lose weight without paying attention to your diet, be aware of the fact that you won't get great results, but rather become Sisyphus' best friend. Eventually, you will end up being dissatisfied because you have not achieved what you expected. You have to think. Of course, education is also important. You can read hundreds of wrong books that won't teach you anything. You can also read many good books and not even try to understand what you have read or understand them but continue doing everything the same way.

It is said that a person is productive for three to four hours a day. The rest of the day usually only involves automated processes. Work, eat, sleep, defecate. A country, I believe it is Sweden, has decided to reduce the number of working days per week from five to four, hoping that people will be more productive in those four days. I do not agree with that statement, superficially speaking, without delving deeper into the analysis at this moment. Why is that?

Obviously, the shortened working week of four days benefits the employee, who will appreciate it. However, one must not ignore who the workers are to whom this service is being provided. In this era of migration and emigration, most of the people in Sweden are not born Swedes but foreigners who simply do not have the same mentality nor share the same values as people born in that country, so they may 'abuse' that benefit given to them because they do not share the same viewpoints as those who have implemented it. However, that is not the topic at hand. Was this communicated properly as a benefit or was it presented as a shortened work week in order to increase worker productivity? In my country, there is a saying that goes: "You cannot pay me as little as little I can work." I do not justify this attitude; I just point out that such an attitude exists. It prevails in the countries that used to have socialist political systems.

So, now what? Now it is necessary to determine the driving force that will increase productivity, not idleness. People can be more productive if they enjoy what they do, if they are involved in decision-making processes, are motivated to come to work, and give their maximum effort. People should live for the company they work for and the team they play for at all times and that can be achieved by making their work environment pleasant, not by shortening their working hours. Even the so-called 'empty desk' mobbing is widely recognized in legal practices. Insufficient engagement and involvement of colleagues in the work process are considered mobbing. I remember the example of a Frenchman who the company wanted to protect because he had some work-related injury, so they didn't give him too much work to do, and he, being a cheeky fellow, sued the same company for mobbing after a few years because his job became monotonous and boring. Given that the company did not give him challenging tasks, he was subjected to mobbing. I'm not getting into who's right or wrong, I'm just emphasizing that people want to work, but they also want to rest and enjoy their work. I despise the fact that in the 21st century, we have abandoned the achievements of the workers' rights advocates from the late 19th century: eight hours of work, eight hours of rest, and eight hours of cultural education. Where are we now, in the 21st century? Who cares about culture, hobbies... Who needs sleep? Do we just need to work?

They say that when you do something you don't like and it burns you out, that's called stress, but when you do something that you love and you give it your all, that's called passion. Someone will say, well, all players love playing that sport, that's why they're doing it. That's true, but not in every team, not in every place, not with the people they don't get along with, not in an atmosphere that doesn't suit them. Do everything to make the players and employees love what they're doing for that team or company. You will achieve this not by preventing them from working, but by enabling them to love their job, to have a good work atmosphere, to be respected and appreciated by managers, to work and sing equally. If we don't understand this, then as employers, managers, bosses, we are in huge trouble. That's our job. And don't confuse it with micro-management, it's not the same thing. Your job is not only to ensure that work is carried out procedurally without any glitches, but also to ensure that your employees smile and are satisfied, not just because it will make them feel more comfortable, nicer and more fun at work, but because your employees will be more productive, so it will be better and nicer for you too. Otherwise, hire robots and machines, which I support, because machines will never, or at least not in the foreseeable future, be able to perform the part of the job that involves reason, or the part of the job that will create higher value of the process, service, or product, so if you can do without human reason, go ahead. They will manage the programmed part of the job fantastically, but you won't get more than that. In order for the company and team to develop day by day, to scale its business, you will have to focus on these 'slaves', I meant to say, robots, oh, workers, players, on a human level, with a full dose of empathy so that you understand them, help them to be better. The beauty is that the better they get for themselves, the better they are for you. You'll see.

Benefits

The Covid era has taken its toll in every aspect, both physically and mentally. Unfortunately, a large number of people have suffered from the consequences of Covid, and may those who have died from the virus rest in peace. In my surroundings, there have been a great number of such cases. Now that Covid is ending, a potential new world war is looming. In light of recent global events, we are witnessing an unprecedented change of self-proclaimed social media epidemiological experts to the most knowledgeable military analysts.

I am not talking about this from the perspective of global conspiracy theories, but rather about controlling workers and players. Until now, the favorite model of control has been when a young football player joins a big club and is 'assigned' a designated club girlfriend, who would usually become his future wife and through whom the club could easily manipulate and control the player. These are public secrets, which are actually no longer secrets. Everything has become public. "Bring shame back to society!" I shout again. Now there is also a controlled workforce that is manipulated through loans; people have to work for low wages so that they wouldn't be left without homes. All these are instruments of control. However, these abused tools can be genuinely used for noble purposes.

A company can build its own building, of course if it has the means; then, it can sell the apartments to its employees at very favorable prices or offer loans on very favorable terms. That is a true benefit for both the worker and the company. The worker knows how difficult it is to find a good mortgage for a house, and the fact that the company has made it possible for him under these conditions will be highly appreciated, while on the other hand, the company is not at a loss. It has certainly earned from the sale of the apartment and has freed itself from the worry that these people will easily leave the company someday.

Wise people try to make the stream flow towards their mill. Someone abuses the same instruments while someone else nobly bestows them for the benefit of all of us. What's the catch? The catch is in realizing what your intentions are. If you want to misuse the situation, you will push your employees into debt, thereby into slavery so that, with your dictatorship, you get an army of obedient and compliant people. Do you really want such a scenario? Do you really think that this way of doing business will go unnoticed and that this way of leading a business is sustainable in the long run? Furthermore, is there any room for development in such conditions, which should come from the employee himself? Even dictators have paid for such attitudes with being removed from power, and here you have an even tougher opponent. On the one hand, such business practices will tarnish your reputation with your employees, with the players who are the game changers, while on the other hand, the market will eat you up because your team needs to work together and strive to bring your company to success, to make a difference in the market, to show what your unique selling point is.

As a wise employer, you can offer all of these things as a benefit, rather than as a necessary evil. This way, you will show your employee how much you care about them and, in return, you will receive their happiness, which will indirectly and directly lead to immeasurable positive results for you and your team. Offer them something without directly asking for a counter-service in the form of loan repayments and debt bondage. The British Empire realized that independent India, a country not under their direct rule, would be more significant to them than bleeding it dry. They gained more by giving more. Evil has never brought any good to anyone. Therefore, make sure to respect the worker, respect the player, and they will reward you generously. Of course, there are also rotten apples among people, they are everywhere, but do not let them be an excuse for you to become trash; instead, see it as an inevitability and as an exception, not as a rule. If you have such rotten apples in your basket, try to get rid of them as soon as possible so that they do not spoil the entire basket. You have to be determined. Strict, but fair. Compassionate, but not merciful. As an owner, manager, boss, leader, or any other person in charge, there is only one thing you need to be above all else: a human being.

Behind the Scenes

The team received medals, they won first place in some competition, they triumphed in the tournament and one by one, they all lined up to hang their hard-earned symbols. They started putting golden medals on their heroic chests. Everyone came out one by one, the coach, the assistant coach, and those you regularly saw on the field and some you had never seen before. 'Who are you guys? What storm has brought you here to the throne with these knights? Nobody has ever seen or heard of you, and now you're here to parade with these heroes who left their hearts on the field.' Didn't we say that it's all teamwork and that success isn't just the result of those we constantly see on small screens, but also an army of people who stand behind the whole endeavor? From the club's gatekeeper to the president of the board of directors, they all contributed in their own way, and it's not just a cliché, it's really like that. What the company reflects is right there at the entrance, at the information desk, in the tidy hallways and offices, in the smiles of those people, not only in relation to the client but also in their communication with each other. All that energy, all that effort at the micro and pico level is woven into the success we see in the end. All these are integral parts of that grandiose success, not only the big ones but also the daily successes and small achievements that everyone accomplishes for the benefit of the entire company.

You have watched a movie, any movie, surely you have. At the beginning of the screening, you see listed all the main production companies, directors, all the main actors, all the important ones, because that's how it should be and is appropriate, while at the end of the screening, when everyone wants to get up and out and quickly head home, while removing popcorn and crumbs from themselves, collecting empty water and juice containers, then comes the part where the names of all those who participated in the creation of that artwork are shown. There you have those who were lighting operators, the main cameramen, and those who carried the lights and the camera, you even have drivers. Drivers! Of course. They also made their contribution, but few are those who want to acknowledge them. Intentionally or unintentionally, everyone wants to see only the most important ones, only their idols. Finally, movie producers have come up with the way to do something about it. To make those invisible people visible, since they know how important those people are to the project and want to show it to others. They have come up with a beautiful solution to put parts of the sequel of that movie or some interesting scenes that could not be integrated into the movie for some reason at the end of the credits, so that everyone who wants to see them has to go through the entire credits and read who is responsible for the realization of this film before they get to the additional scenes. When you have read everything, who did what, we will show you additional scenes. Only those who have gone through the entire credits will be rewarded with those scenes.

Recently, in our company, we got a fantastic idea that we decided to realize through shooting a promotional video. I really wanted it to be, like this book, a homemade product, created by the company people. It wasn't supposed to be a professional video, rather a way to pull people out of their comfort zones, to have them as actors and extras. Those who know how to film would direct, and come up with the whole project to the best of their ability. In the end, it would be a product of our own hands, and we would all be proud of it and always enjoy watching it, sharing it, and showing it to others. And it really was like that. Everyone contributed, some more, some less, but everyone tried their best. The promotional video with our people, supporting our business partners, sports, and the national team, turned out just as it should have. I am so proud of everyone. My heart is full. I was asked who had worked on the project, and I was taken aback. It was a completely legitimate question, but I was confused. What should I say? I started listing names, but then I thought to myself that if I started naming people, there was a possibility that I might leave someone out. Everyone contributed, the whole company. My response was, 'Everyone.' How could everyone be involved? Well, everyone, both those you see in the movie and those you don't, those who directly participated and those who didn't. Everyone took part in this endeavor, everyone.

There are economists and water carriers, and they are all part of that team. Of course, there are also the benchwarmers. These people aren't just there to step in when someone from the starting lineup gets injured; they are there to contribute to the team. Each of them has their own task. There's even a third goalie. A third goalie! This person has never played in an official match. They signed a contract saying that they would be, not the second but exclusively the third goalie. What's the point of having them? That third goalie has their own value, and it's a big one. He will practice actions, tactics, work on his physical fitness during training sessions. By working on himself, he indirectly helps his teammates. With his effort, he will inspire the second and first goalkeepers to be even better than they are. Healthy competition arises. Thus, he directly and indirectly affects the performance of the entire team. During the game, he cheers on his teammates, puts pressure on the referees, waves the towel, confuses the opponent, and communicates with the fans. He is always an essential part of the folklore of every game. And should he receive a medal, even though he hasn't set foot on the pitch? Yes, he should, and he should receive a reward because he deserves it, even if his direct contribution was not immediately recognized.

What about the audience popularly known as the twelfth player? Should they receive a medal too? Yes, they should. They will celebrate without a medal because the club's success is their success, but I will not write about the audience because if I start writing about them, I will have to write a whole new book.

Shortsightedness

The late owner of 'DM drogerie markt' retail store chain, Götz Werner, who managed to create a business empire, was a man who gifted his company not to his children, but to a charitable foundation, saying 'It's not shameful to become rich, but it's shameful to die rich'. This has also been advocated by Bill Gates and most billionaires, but I don't want to discuss the accuracy of their statements, I want to emphasize that Mr. Werner was consistent and realized it. It's not about what he did at the end, but about what he did and accomplished during his life. When there were recessions, he did not reduce salaries, but increased them. When toothpaste manufacturers decided to sell smaller packages at the same prices as the larger ones, they publicly protested in their stores right next to the shelves where these products were displayed, warning customers that DM was on the side of the customer, not on the side of profit. But the most significant thing was his attitude that every person, every worker, every player on the stage of life must have enough money to live a normal life, not to worry about bills and a roof over their heads. When the worker has that, then he will return it many times over to the employer because he will no longer be afraid for their bare existence, but will focus more on their job and be more productive. They will not live in fear of how to make it through tomorrow, but will give more and more. They will repay. Now, there are also ungrateful ones. Those should be immediately dismissed from the company. So, why isn't that a common practice among employers? Excellent question. Perhaps everyone thinks that people give their maximum when they are under pressure without being given a choice. It is possible that they consider freedom of thought to be the devil's work in this day and age, so they don't allow people, not even for a second, to raise their voice and awaken their reason. It is also possible that they don't know how to deal with others' opinions, fearing that those might harm them first and foremost, rather than the company. It is possible that they are afraid of unionization. I would rather say that the basis for this is that most managers have built their image on fear and respect, on boss-like foundations, because it is easier and simpler that way. No one can ask you anything, everyone listens without questions asked, there is no room for weaknesses to show. In such an environment, there is no room for creativity or progress, but it is easy to 'rule'. The iron fist is a proven historical practice. And everyone shares this opinion, but everyone forgets that all those who 'ruled' like that have ended their time in power very quickly. On the other hand, most managers are careerists, so they don't really care that much. They come, apply their regular recipe, usually succeed, but only in the short term. They will take their salary, their bonuses, and after a few years at best, they will leave behind a wasteland. You don't build a house like that, my dear ones. But if careerists do it, why do entrepreneurs do it the same way? The only explanation is that, instead of being led by success and prosperity, they are, in the vast majority of cases, led by profit. The sooner, the better. The end justifies the means. Very few can see even a couple of years ahead. It's a shame. They shoot themselves in the foot. Teams and companies are not led that way. They are not led by profit, but by development and prosperity.

The path of leadership is harder. It is truly more demanding and responsible. It is harder to descend among people, workers, players, and show them how much they mean to you. To show that you eat the same bread, that their success is your success, that you know and acknowledge that you depend on them. It is harder, more exhausting. How much energy is needed to build authority without bossing around, without questioning, without showing weakness! It is harder, but it is more productive. You have plenty of opportunities. You create a team, a unity. You create such an atmosphere that when something goes downhill, those people will not leave you the way rats leave a sinking ship; they will be there to share both good and bad with you. Oh, how much energy it takes, how much sacrifice! Well, you need skill for that. You have to learn, develop, improve, and breathe that way of life. The other option is easier. You divide tasks, so if something goes wrong in the field, it's not your fault, it's the workers' fault, it's the players' fault, and your responsibility ends when you issue tasks. Few people think beyond that, and that leads to endless excuses for not completing assigned tasks. Everyone in the chain shifts responsibility onto the one below or, at best, beside them, and we know the epilogue. Collapse. Not quite so great working conditions. Those who think even a little bit with their own heads begin to question their role and place in that company. They look for their place in the value coordinate system, start measuring themselves and others, and as a rule, they leave such an environment. They stop advocating in the field and look at when and where to escape as far away from such a way and treatment of the worker and work itself. And the market is no longer a pond, it has now become as global as never before. They can work for whomever they want to, especially now in the time of remote work. The market will harshly regulate everything. All things will fall into place eventually. The lucky ones will reach it sooner, while the less fortunate will have to make more effort to reach such clubs. But they will come, at least those who know what they are looking for. It has always been true that every pot finds its lid, every hole its patch, although it happens that there is no cap for someone named Rajko, but those cases are rare. I would rather say that the problem is with Rajko, not the cap. Whoever looks for something will find it. Dreams tend to come true, so be careful what you wish for, it might surprise you.

I Came with a Purpose

Why is it that a girl who wasn't born and raised in the city she currently lives in always sings louder in the tavern and wears a shorter skirt than those who were born in that city? It's because she doesn't carry the burden of reputation. Nobody knows her there, so she feels freer. I always find an analogy in that little skirt when I see the desire in those players who came from smaller towns to a big city searching for a better life and an opportunity to play for a big club. They left their town or even homeland behind and burned all the bridges and are more determined to achieve their goals. They are the ones that employers need, those players who give the maximum of their abilities because they don't have the comfort of a safe harbor. They don't have a brilliant backup option. They will endure everything.

And it is often that these people become victims of greedy employers. They blackmail, belittle, and keep them in financial uncertainty. Such employers love them the most. The wise ones respect diligent people because they know how hardworking, valuable, and dedicated to success they are, but the others, the malicious ones, exploit them as if they were trading in white slavery. And there is a solution for that if you are that kind of player. Sit, be quiet, endure, and search for a backup plan, for your chance to escape. It's easy to talk about all of this, but such mental, and sometimes physical torture must be endured. It's not easy, but it's not impossible to find your place under the sky. The important thing is not to give up on that journey. There will always be those who appreciate the player, those who recognize their importance regardless of their current physical shape. Those who understand that in business and in life there are ups and downs. They are aware of the fact that all people make mistakes, but that their attitude and desire for success are crucial. When you come across such a player, embrace them, keep them close as a friend, but do not dull thy palm with entertainment. I'm convinced this is from 'Hamlet'. What do business, sport, and 'Hamlet' have in common? Well, you see, they do have something in common. All those things are imbued with life. Regardless of their business and private nature. It's all life. I spend more time at work than at home. I see colleagues more than I see my own children. It is only natural that I want to be happy and comfortable at work. Of course, I want it to be creative, challenging, and productive. But I don't want my job to be everything in the world to me. I don't want to lose myself in that relationship. I want my job to be inspiring, full of wonderful experiences. See, it's like I'm talking about a love affair. That's what I've been saying all along. Everything is intertwined, everything is connected. All of this is very, very important to everyone in the world, in every corner of the globe. Now, it's up to us how we perceive it. How foolishly we approach our lives, how deeply we analyze them with a desire to change what's not so good and with even greater passion to cultivate good practices, to go from good to great.

The Impostor Syndrome

A player comes to a new club, full of self-confidence and experience, with over a hundred games behind him. He knows his job, but the environment is new, the people are new, everything new surrounding him requires time to adapt and see where he has come to. He needs to "click" with the new team, with new colleagues, adapt to a new tactic, a new manager's strategy, and find his place. The point is not just in the new environment but in the mindset of it. He carries the self-confidence he gained from successful games and a proven track record in his legs. However, a true player knows that not everything has been up to him. He was just one of the team members. The successes he achieved were not only his own but a result of good understanding and implementation of the coach's wishes and ideas and the efforts of his teammates. Now it is a new environment, and as a rule, he does not perform as well. Something is not right here.

The transfer was impressive, and the expectations of the new club are high. He is the one who needs to put everything in order. He is the solution to the problems they had in that position. Pressure is mounting. Somehow, he doesn't get along very well with his teammates. The coach can't seem to do an adequate adaptation and help him fit into the team. He gives him chances, but something just doesn't go as everyone hoped, as everyone wanted. The tension is mounting. Instead of gentle words of understanding from the coach and, perhaps, some teammates, he is not receiving what he really needs, which is a clearly defined goal and how to achieve it. What's not working in the whole story? The self-confidence he came with is slowly melting away like an ice cube on a hot sunny day. Every present moment is now being scrutinized as is the relevance of the past. If this is not resolved soon, real problems will arise. The player is unable to cope with the pressure that, on the one hand, comes from not achieving the desired results, and on the other hand, the harsh media pressures that demand immediate results, thus adding fuel to the fire. Coaches and teammates begin to unconsciously succumb to the influence of the media and the environment. They clumsily try to provide even greater support, but the problem begins to take its toll. The downfall begins.

Am I a fraud? What's wrong? Countless questions and self-doubt arise. The imposter syndrome is at play. The positive side of this syndrome is that it has been identified in modern business. Awareness has been raised that it exists and needs to be dealt with. It arises from unrealistic or insufficiently clear challenges that are posed to the player by the management, while, at the same time, the most common case is that the problem arises from the individual's inability to cope with the demands they place on themselves. A good and hardworking player usually ends up on the losing end in that vortex.

There are many such cases. Sometimes they are irreversible for players. Some never free themselves from that syndrome, while others are reborn through a change of environment or a coach. This leads to the next danger, which is reflected in the tendency to run away and say that things are better somewhere else than where we really are. This syndrome often provides excuses for running away from problems instead of using it to strengthen the individual. There is no perfect solution or scenario. First and foremost, a person needs to be honest with themselves, look in the mirror, and determine whether they have tried hard enough, whether the problem lies with them or their environment. It's like trying to please your partner within the limits of your abilities, but they remain unsatisfied. Both points of view are legitimate. It's perfectly fine to have aspirations and goals in order to achieve the desired result, but it's important to ask oneself whether those goals are realistic. On the other hand, those goals might be realistic, but you might simply not be up to the challenge. A happy divorce is better than an unhappy marriage. Each side should take stock of the situation before going their separate ways. They should determine the cause of the problem and whether their expectations were realistic. This is crucial for both parties. From the employer's perspective, it's important to identify where the problem arose so they don't make the same mistake with a new employee, wasting valuable time and resources. From the employee's perspective, it's important to know whether the problem lies with them or the employer's unrealistic expectations. If the problem lies with the employee, they should make an effort to meet the employer's expectations not only in that company or team, but also for future employers, with an emphasis on personal growth.

I've always wondered how some people don't feel responsible for their poor performance and how it doesn't seem to affect them. Well, it's clear that they're not up to the task, and we can all see it, but they still don't have a solution to the problem. Not only do they not have a solution for the same problem, but they are not even aware that they have a problem with poor performance. It's like everything is fine with them. They get paid, and as for the rest of you, who cares. That's your problem, not mine. There are countless examples of this, whether it's in sports, politics, or business. They are everywhere. But the most striking one, in my opinion, is Harry Maguire and others like him, who don't seem to have this problem at all. Here I go again about him! He is a wonderful example. He is not only the most expensive defender in the history of sports, but he is also far above average, and, to top it all off, the captain. He absolutely doesn't acknowledge his own poor performances, or if he does, he certainly doesn't show it. He doesn't show that he has a problem, nor does he show that he is doing anything to solve the evident poor performance. He's my 'idol'. If he could do it, then so can I. Put his picture in sports locker rooms all over the world as the obvious proof that anyone can succeed. I have his picture set as the wallpaper on my mobile phone.

But it happens everywhere. It happens to everyone. No one wants to be in that situation. I believe in people's honesty. Daniel Ricciardo, one of the best Formula 1 drivers, joined the new McLaren team as a big star. He was supposed to support his young teammate Lando Norris. The expectations were high as they should have been. And Ricciardo just couldn't get the hang of the new car. Lando dominated, and Ricciardo just couldn't pull it off. The same car, as the same car, and even if it's not the same, the differences are small. This is not the first time Ricciardo has changed teams he's driving for. So, he is no stranger to changes. Adapting to a new environment is something he is used to. He just can't do it. He can't get used to the new car, and that's it. Sometimes you can give it your all, give everything you have, but there are no results. That's when you need support, to endure, to overcome, to persevere. You need someone to come and tell you what you already know very well, that sometimes it's like that and it's not worth getting upset. That you just need to keep going and everything will be fine.

Two-way Street

If you don't share the same values with the company and the management, it's time for you to pack your bags. There's no way to change that. Changing is not impossible, but fighting against windmills will exhaust you completely. I remember one legendary high school physical education teacher who always had some wisdom to enlighten generations. No matter how much it annoyed me as a teenager at that time, it was always enough to make me wonder. The new generations don't even have teachers who do their job properly, let alone such great personalities who would devote themselves to their students outside of school activities. So, what did my teacher say to me? 'Don't try to change the world. The world will crush you, and you'll lose all your strength, and in the end, you'll be the one at a loss'. And something came to my mind, so I asked him, 'But if I use the strength of the world to achieve my goals, then I'll be a winner, right?' We looked at each other silently, and went our separate way. Today, I think we were both right, but the price that had to be paid with my approach would be definitely too high.

When a player is looking for a new club, he should choose it just as they choose him. It's a two-way process, you know. He studies his employer, his colleagues, his coach. I love that probationary period when the employer evaluates your work, your contribution, your character, and doesn't even realize that he himself is being evaluated. Well, employees evaluate him too, and they look at the company culture, the relationship of the managers with workers, and the relationships among colleagues. They look at the energy within the company itself. If they don't do that, they're in deep water. Then they go blindly forward and accept whatever fate has in store for them. Who wants that kind of scenario? Who wants to be absolutely uninvolved in their own life? When you choose a club or a new work environment where you will play, don't just follow the salary, but do that due diligence that will comprehensively show you all the characteristics of the company that are important to you. It's not all about the money. You have to play for that club, live with those teammates, share good and bad. When the game takes an unwanted turn, you need to support each other, and when you win, you need to know how to celebrate that success. Keep choosing as long as you can choose. If you're not able to choose, try to put yourself in a situation where you can do it in the next iteration. It's true that the possibility of choice is a "curse," but you have to fight for it. Try to protect yourself from wrong choices because they cost too much. They cost time and money, but they also cost nerves. Of course, you'll make mistakes, you'll have bad judgments, but that's all part of the job, part of life. Every step you take is a learning opportunity, but make it a meaningful one.

The coach has a plan that he wants you to implement on the field, and in your opinion, yours is a complete opposite. At this point, it doesn't matter who is right. If you are there as a player, your task is to implement the coach's desire and take care of the proper execution of the job. Otherwise, you undermine the team, undermine the coach's credibility. You harm the team, and. by doing that you harm yourself. On the other hand, the coach's idea may have a dimension that you cannot see from your perspective. When you become a coach, then you can implement your own ideas, but until then, do what is expected of you. As a rule, players like that are quickly removed from the team. Goodbye and good luck. If you are that player, think carefully before starting with such behavior. Now you know the outcome for certain.

A Guy for Everything

Real leaders know how to help their players find the appropriate place in the team. They are there to assess and evaluate what is best for both the player and the team. Experienced fighters come to new challenges, carrying a wealth of experience, and with a new team, they receive new tasks. They adapt to a new formation, new demands from the coach, which conceptually differ from everything they have done before. They are students who come from youth schools or young talents from developing countries or, as the developed countries call us, from the third-world countries, in search of affirmation, fame, and, in all cases, wealth. They have played in some lower leagues in the world and are now coming to try their luck with the best and strongest. Playing in smaller clubs, they managed to reach their maximum potential there. Quite often they would leave their heart on the field trying to prove their worth while, at the same time, they were immature as both players and people. More often than not, young footballers were noticed for their incredible performances, then got hired by some big teams and when they arrived there they were completely lost. There were exceptions, of course. They set out in search of fame and wealth and instead of taking small steps by playing in smaller clubs, learning and consolidating the basics, they bit the biggest apple and then choked on it just like Snow White.

The job of a good coach is to adequately guide these kids, as well as those in the prime of their youth, to provide them with an easier transition and adaptation period, which is always difficult. A new player comes to the club and starts doing what he does best, but the coach doesn't need that. What this player has done before simply doesn't fit in with his concept. He was brought for something else, not to play the same game with new teammates at the same level as he did in his former club. New circumstances, new challenges, it is understandably difficult. The learning process continues, everything is fine. The wise quickly absorb new knowledge, the slightly duller ones stick to the old ways and end up somewhere at the back of everyone's mind. The resourceful ones quickly adapt, diligently learn, practice, and everything slowly falls into place. But the situation in the club changes due to constant injuries, layoffs, player sales, and new positions need to be filled for the team to function. They take on roles they never dreamed of. Left-backs become right or central defenders. Central defenders become offensive players. Defenders become attackers. Attackers become defenders, and all combinations are open when the situation calls for it. But usually, these temporary measures are of a permanent nature. And in the end, you become a guy for everything. A universal soldier. Indeed, it is an honor to have such giants in your teams who can replace any player. To provide top-notch performances in any given position, but as a rule, these players never reach their full potential. They never become the best football players who do their job best. They become and remain the best substitutes. Now, let's not deceive ourselves, that's an honor, primarily given by the coach who believes you will finish any task that is set before you. That's good for the team, truth to be told, but it's not good for an individual. Especially if this temporary measure of a permanent nature prolongs and you are in those positions at the expense of your development, that is, improvement for what you want to play; it can lead to a big problem. You're not doing what you know and can do, not to mention that you're not doing what you love. You weren't preparing for these tasks, and now you're doing multiple jobs. And there's no specialization. And if there's no specialization, then there's no fantastic success. There are also those situations, which are the worst, where someone has to play in certain positions because otherwise there wouldn't be a place for them in the team. And frustrations and dissatisfaction begin. But why? You're your coach's ace. The golden boy who solves everything. Not because he wants to but because he has to do the solving. Has anyone asked that golden boy if he likes the role assigned to him? Maybe they have. And he said he understood the situation and would give his best for the team's needs, but it's not something he wanted to develop in. Everyone looks at the goal, but neglects the player. There are new challenges, new narrowly specialized players who take over the positions that universal soldier wanted to play in. That was his wish, where he wanted to improve, but the coach needed something else. There will be time, he will wait for his turn.

As one of my friends would say, everyone would take me to a desert island with them to help out because God made me so versatile and skilled. He was born for everything, but in the labor market, he just can't seem to find the right fit. He has a little bit of everything, but nothing specific. Everything is a job for him, but he can never seem to get paid what he deserves. He's everyone's favorite and is really hardworking, but he is never appreciated as he should be because he is not specialized in what he does. He's everywhere, yet nowhere. That's really problematic in the real world. Let's take an example of dating five girls at the same time. The number is taken entirely at random, and I have to admit that I haven't faced such challenges in my life. You give them all a piece of your attention, but not enough. You haven't fully given yourself to any of them. The epilogue is self-evident. All five will be dissatisfied. What do you do then? You have to replace those five dissatisfied girls with five new ones because the situation demands it. Also, if you continue with the same practice, the result will be the same. What can you change? I mean, in terms of approach with those five chosen ones who have the privilege of being in your company. You need to choose not three, not two, but only one from those five who will be your chosen one. The one who will have all your love and attention. And in the end, you'll end up with her, in a happy marriage until the end of your life. But let's not get into that now. If you once stray from the goal you set for yourself, as a rule, only you can return to that path. Your coach can only show you the way you need to go, you are the one who has to cross that distance. Your legs have to do the walking. There will always be those who want to help you, and there will be others who won't, but it's your life you're living. Your decisions are what you make or don't make.

The saying "A jack of all trades is a master of none, but oftentimes better than a master of one" is often used. They say it was referring to William Shakespeare. He could do anything around the stage, scenery, costumes, and finally, by acquiring all his knowledge and skills, he decided to specialize. He decided to become one of the greatest writers of all time. Learn all the knowledge and absorb it. Take care of your time and energy. And when you feel that the moment has come and you possess the adequate breadth, start your specialization.

If you are stuck in a position in a company that you don't care about and don't want to work in, it will certainly create enormous anxiety. Insecurity will arise, but perhaps new horizons will open up. Something that you couldn't see on your own until now. In that position, you have to improve and specialize, but always make sure that the choice is yours alone. Just because you know how to do something doesn't mean it's what you want to do.

Out of Sight, Out of Mind

You bring a child to the club, but either they're too young, and you don't want to deal with them, or you bought them just because it was a fantastic business opportunity, not because you really needed them. Or you bring in a good player, and they turn out to be useless. What are your options? The option with the overpaid player is to send them on loan somewhere else so they don't ruin the atmosphere in the team or warm the bench. You send them somewhere to fill in a vacant place or just to keep fit, trying to improve them somewhere in the big world. Let's be honest, they weren't viable for you. They're getting paid, but you're not getting any benefit from them. And some guy, your colleague, will shape them just the way you need them and send them back to you. Yeah, right. That guy will never return to their home club that sent them somewhere else. As a rule, they either find happiness in their new club or return to their home club, which either loans them out again or sells them to someone else. These guys never play for their home club. And why would they? The club subtly told them they weren't good enough for them, but they would create an opportunity so that somebody else could waste time with them because we have more important and smarter things to do.

Then there's the other situation when you buy young players, preferably still in diapers, who will show their potential in the future. It looks like legalized human trafficking to me as a layman. Let me not be so harsh, but I find this practice disgusting. I don't know if it's more nauseating that these vultures try, and often succeed, in picking up talented children and promising them a bright future someday, somewhere, or the parents of these children who are willing to sacrifice their children's childhoods in pursuit of their own dreams and see them only as money-making machines.

And you bring these kids into your youth boarding schools and gather so many of them that you don't know what to do with them. You buy even those your scouts said were okay. You even buy those who have been identified by your competitors, just so that they wouldn't get them. You benefit at the expense of others. It's a ruthless game of large amounts and unscrupulous market dealings. But let's get back to those kids. And now you push them into all your possible youth schools. You send them to other clubs. They play for your 14th team, then for the B team. If I hadn't read those magazines at betting shops, I wouldn't even know how many B teams these big clubs have. They can have their own leagues. Then you allow them to play with the best ones, the first team, just to make them feel the atmosphere. To learn from your best first-team players. Then something completely different happens. You send them off to some other, friendly club, for training, because they're not good enough for yours, where a colleague of yours continues working with them.

First of all, there's no such thing as continuing your work, because that guy there will shape them to suit his own needs, not yours. He might instill a mindset that is exactly what you don't want, what you don't cultivate, what you don't support. Boy, oh boy, the number of business examples like this! It's terrifying. The moment that young man left you and started adopting someone else's values, he can hardly be useful to you later on. That's when he starts to form his mindset. And you leave that to others?! You're casting pearls before swine, but that is always justified by business decisions. Whose business? For whose sake? Well, it's not that bad, they could have just thrown him away.

Better this way. You've already ruined his childhood. What more can be done?

And you kids, why are you skipping the steps? I understand that it's a necessity of modern times, but if you're skipping them, don't forget that you'll have to come back to those lessons that you've skipped. Not everything is about instant success. You're much more than that. Out of sight, out of mind. No long-distance relationship has ever lasted, except perhaps few, but as a rule, they don't succeed. Let's not even get into whys and hows. You're far from the base. You weren't there when decisions were made, you weren't there when they celebrated, nor when they cried. You're somewhere far away, but a part of the team? Yeah, right. And pigs can fly!

How can that player share the values of his home club? How can he reach his maximum potential? It's impossible. He can develop his skills at an average level there, but he won't reach the pinnacle of his professional life. It's okay to train people out of sight, but that shouldn't last long. It's like relocating a job to a third-world country where labor is cheaper. I have nothing against it, unless the working conditions there are inhumane. If you move the operational part of your business there, you can't relocate development there. You do know that, right? So, if you're aware of that, how is it that you don't understand that you can't expect those people there to be wizards in their work? They'll be doing some simple jobs, not too complicated, and you can develop what you want at home. Development is at home, and you can outsource simpler jobs.

If you don't get smoked, you don't get warmed. As a player, you have to be aware of the sacrifice you're making, but with a clear goal that should always be in front of your eyes. Smoke and tears in your eyes aside, there must be a clear vision why you're making that sacrifice. It must be constantly in front of your eyes, otherwise you're doing everything in vain. You have to be close to the source of learning, close to influential managers, not some lower-level guys who wouldn't even be where they are now if they were better and more valued in their work. It's hot by the fire and you can easily get burned, but if you're not close, well, good luck with frostbite!

Onboarding

When those new kids come into that new environment, they are scared. Even the experienced and the old ones are scared, not just the kids. They need to be meaningfully reassured. They need to be encouraged and empowered. All their fears, doubts, and uncertainties must be removed. Fear can be overwhelming. Everything is new, unknown. It's a terrifying feeling. Those first impressions can bring so much wrong that you have to prepare very well for their arrival. Nowadays, it's called the onboarding process. If companies don't already have that process developed, then they're in big trouble. The problem lies in the fact that not only will it be harder and more complicated for those people to adapt to the new system and corporate culture, and for you to employ them at full capacity after a sea of troubles, but also in the fact that you can permanently lose them. If they don't find their way immediately, if they don't have proper guidance, some of them, being so frightened, can even develop a permanent discomfort towards the new environment. What can be done? Well, it's always better to be safe than sorry.

A new person comes into your company and no matter how experienced they are in their job, no matter how many times they've gone through it, they simply feel a certain discomfort. So, one of the first rules, for those who deal with public speech, regardless of the number of years they have spent making presentations, is to get acquainted with the space in which they perform. It's simply necessary to feel the new spirit, the new atmosphere, the new smell that the new company carries. And we all know that almost all singers, actors, and other public figures have stage fright and publicly admit it. It usually disappears after the first sentence, but it is present before that sentence is uttered. It exists. What can be done to alleviate it as much as possible?

I am always reminded of a fact that, unfortunately, in some companies new people are often left on self-onboarding. They stumble upon them in the hallways and everyone avoids them. The famous approach is that the new person needs to make a list of questions and then go to a supervisor to resolve them. But onboarding is a continuous process. It is not just about questions and answers; it is much more sophisticated. It requires a systematic and comprehensive approach. And what happens to such people in the end? What else can they do but pack up and seek happiness elsewhere.

Focus on people when they decide to start their lives in your company. If you don't have an onboarding process, build it, and then start implementing and upgrading it. Even tourist attractions have guides, and you should at least make an effort to have a dedicated person who would introduce newcomers to the basics of house rules. There are fears, doubts, whether it was the right decision, how I will find my way round. All of this needs to be understood and worked on so that the individual can overcome it as soon as possible. Then focus on people in those first few days, as they need your humane assistance the most. You must introduce them to your team's way of working as soon as possible, so that it is clearly defined what is expected of them and what their specific tasks are. What they need to work on, what to pay attention to. Otherwise, everything is in vain. On the other hand, these players must be interested in their own fate and lives. They must seek and recognize their responsibilities. They must be aware that they need to adapt to the new environment. They must give themselves individual tasks. They must self-organize in such a way that they can also adapt to the new environment as well and as quickly as possible. They did not come here on vacation. They came to work, to show what they can do, to prove themselves. The team is a complex environment, as is the company. That machinery must always be functional. All screws must be in place. Everything must work perfectly. And even then, the result is uncertain. But if this is not present, failure is guaranteed. There are many flaws in all companies. There is no one to welcome them properly, to direct them, and then we come to the point where these players say 'we don't have anyone to work with here', turn around and leave. Some do it out of ambition, some out of vanity, some because they have a better offer, but they all have one thing in common, they did not feel welcome, respected by the company. Even guests are welcomed when they cross your doorstep. If such people were not needed then, why did you bring them into your ranks in the first place? To waste their and your time? So that after that, they have every right to characterize you as an undesirable employer? Of course, there are a million reasons to confirm their claim, as well as to refute it. Nothing is black and white, but if you are an employer, respect the worker, and if you are an employee, try as much as you can, too. In both cases, that is how it is done. And, above all, it is humane.

Far Away from Here

There has always been a question about the experience, or rather the quality, of the players who make up a team. This topic always reminds me of the eternal struggle over outsourcing the workforce to India. With all due respect to all Indians, Pakistanis, Belarusians, and all recognized developers around the world, I still believe that the development of all advanced product functionalities needs to be done in-house, at the base. Less demanding and less responsible tasks can be done remotely, but the core of the business should be left under close supervision, near the central hub. I would rather say that this has nothing to do with the region where the outsourcing process takes place, but with the people who make up and lead that team far away, without, perhaps, the most adequate control and guidance. It is cost effective, no question about it. Also, there is no doubt about their being wise, smart, and capable of doing any task that is given to them. They can and will do it, but... the final product is not always what you envisioned in the first place. It's like watching a chef prepare a dish. You watch what he does, he is right next to you, nothing hidden, no lies. He takes an ingredient, and you take it too. He does something, you do the same thing. You prepare it in the same way, knead it the same way, mix it the same way, and he prepares the dish, and you prepare it too. His is top-notch, and yours doesn't even come close. How is that possible? That's the story. We do everything the same, we make everything the same, but the product never seems to turn out the way the best and greatest expert would make it, even though the recipe is exactly the same. It's just not the same as when you would do it.

For such outsourcing jobs, you always have to build a strong base of people to lead them. You invest so much in the operational management to adequately oversee and lead those remote teams so that when you sum it all up, it would cost you less if you had paid more for developers at home than creating that multifunctional super team in the home country that needs to lead those people somewhere far away. There are also phenomenal examples that don't fit into this story, but as I have mentioned many times before, beauty is in the eye of the beholder.

So now you are faced with a challenge. It slaps you in the face every day. How do you put together that mechanism of people that you have or don't have, but have a desire to have, and want it to be exactly as you wanted and imagined in your head? Do you hire seniors who will handle more demanding tasks, but cost an arm and a leg, or do you do it all with some fresh-faced college students or recent graduates? If those kids could make it as seniors could, that would be a winning combination. It costs less and it's easier to work with them. They don't nitpick or act like they know everything. They keep quiet, endure, and learn. But what kind of product will come out in the end? Will it be satisfactory? Difficult, if not impossible to say. So, you have to make some combinations. Some old people, some young, or all of them to be somewhere in the middle? The truth is somewhere in between, of course. When I say in between, I don't mean the recipe that exists. To be more to the point 'The truth is out there'. It's necessary to be wise and to assess each team member separately. To find him the appropriate place in the team, where he can contribute the most and the best, but also be satisfied himself. If he is doing well, the company will do well too.

I have always been a supporter of bringing in young players and indoctrinating them from an early age, but you cannot expect such people to have ten years of experience when they are only around twenty years old. I still find it funny that there was a job ad that required five years of experience in some programming language. The person who invented that programming language commented publicly on the ad and said, 'It's hard to find someone who has worked with that program for five years. I invented it three years ago'. Well, today ads are written by HR people without consulting with the department head, hence the error, and I won't comment on that. Nonetheless, it's an example that always makes me laugh.

You have senior developers whose role would be to lead the work and solve the most demanding tasks. They would just have to take a look at a part of the code and everything would be solved with that one look. Believe it or not, it happens, but more often in movies and rumors than in reality. But it does happen. That senior, however, is fed up with coming to work. He would like to set himself some different challenges. They all talk about being eager for new knowledge. They have forgotten that they have been saying the same thing since the end of their studies. What new knowledge can you gain at 45 years of age as a developer? That story works when you are young, when it is the perfect excuse to change teams or companies. I don't have enough challenges here, so I have to look for my happiness somewhere else. Maybe your current employer can buy your new desires and challenges with a higher salary, or maybe another club can offer you a higher salary to play in their team, under the pretext of learning new technologies there. Now that you're a senior, you want to rest, not to be up to your ear in work. But wouldn't it be best to pass on your knowledge and experience to younger generations? To change the way they think, not to solve their problems for them, but to teach them how to approach and solve problems correctly. To gently guide them in the right direction. Or will you jealously keep your knowledge to yourself and not share it with anyone? If you don't feel the need to share knowledge selflessly with colleagues, someone should point that out to you. To lead you in the right direction. And the young ones should, like puppies, follow that old dog, watch him, learn how to think.

Was Matt Busby right when he put together a team of 'babies' and destroyed the English league? Yes. Did anyone else succeed after that? Yes. Did many try after him? Yes. Did most of them succeed? No. So there is no exact recipe for success. There are desirable models, but there is no recipe for guaranteed success. It is wonderful to help young people develop and it is highly desirable, but those kids need a guide besides their own bravery to show them how to 'hold their horses'. Someone who will lead them through success with their wisdom. Someone who will encourage them after failure. Because life is like that, it goes up and down. Assemble a team of experienced devils and young angels and lead them. Lead them all the time. Lead the old ones too. Just because they are old doesn't mean they are invulnerable. It doesn't mean they don't need guidance, too. They fall too, but when they fall, their bones break, that's old age. Help them understand and get along with each other. Help them to be better. Don't lead their battles for them, because they're not yours, but teach them how to fight. Let them make mistakes. Teach them to respect both colleagues and opponents. To be great in victory and defeat. Lead them and teach them how to become good and honest people, and they will repay you a hundredfold.

Work Begets Work, and Idleness Begets Idleness Begin

I don't know why I so often remember what I learned, heard or acquired in high school. Surely, the young brain has the greatest absorptive power then. It accumulates a number of beautiful and useful things, and as a bonus, along comes such foolishness that sometimes it outweighs and has the potential to lead you astray. That's why I say that it's very responsible and demanding to work with young people. At that time, I encountered my first intellectual conversations, philosophies, not to mention that I belong to that generation of hyperinflation, wars, and the bombing of the "Merciful Angels". Oh, then in high school, you start reading and hearing slightly different stories for the first time. Then come the philosophies based on the principle of 'Which wolf do you feed?', whether you do the right things, and so on and so forth. They still follow me today. But no matter what we did, no matter what we read, we somehow kept chasing our tails and returning to what my math teacher, who taught us lazy students, always said: "Work begets work, and idleness begets idleness."

Be dedicated and consistent, and you can hope for something good. Otherwise, you are doomed to mediocrity and failure. I really have nothing against mediocrity, in fact, I hold it so close to my heart, but it just won't grow on me. Mediocrity means I'm satisfied with myself. I'm where I am, and I don't want to be better. I just want everyone to leave me alone. Well, it won't work. Because that's when you become a target. They just can't leave you alone. Why did nature arrange it that way, and believe me that it's because of nature, not you? When you're satisfied with where you are and don't want to be better, you think you've reached the desired level and that you'll stay there. Reality, however, is a bit different from what you imagine. What's the worst that can happen to you? That you stagnate? You think you're stagnating, but in reality, you're regressing. Everything around you is developing, progressing, changing, and you're starting to be swallowed and slowly eroded by the ravages of time, without even noticing it. It is natural, or rather mandatory, that you must constantly work on yourself, that you must try day in and out. If you sit and do nothing, vultures will come and start tearing apart your body, thinking you're dead. When you feel the first slap of life in that comatose state, you'll wake up. And then you start, but with a delayed start. Your opponents have already moved on. You'll have to try harder. You start from the mud. They are not enemies who oppress you, but the natural order of those who do not sleep. They are the ones who follow their natural animal instinct for self-development and of course, the ones who are overambitious, who have bitten more than they can chew.

Constant improvement has been imposed on us by Mother Nature, as well as those malicious ones who are the integral part of it. Some say that young generations will come and trample you. Whether they will trample you or not depends solely on you, but they will come for sure. You can be bored, fall, rest, crawl, tear yourself to pieces, even fall asleep for a second, but you must not be a sleeping beauty. Therefore, you must not be mediocre. I'm sorry. That utopia doesn't exist. You don't need to be the best in the world. You need to be something much, much, much more. You need to be better than yourself.

Inevitability of Improvement

I often go out for a walk with my wife. We make sure to maintain this wonderful practice of walking and being silent. How beautifully silent we are together! Sometimes one of us says something. Jokes aside, fruitful silence is just as good as the best conversation. I have always had this unwritten rule, and now I'm writing it down, that I choose my company based on how comfortable I am being silent with someone. In that silence and in those conversations, various topics naturally arise. Like medicine for the soul. And the topic of personal and professional development, of human improvement, inevitably arose. I, unrelentingly realistic, told my lady that I'd noticed a very confusing fact about the change in the quality of the workforce in the market. I look at myself and say, I've been trying all this time, maybe not enough, in my opinion, to be better with every day, in life and in work. Let's just talk about work now. What could have fruitfully influenced my professional development? What is it that pushes me, that drives me to be better, to be of better quality to myself and to others? I've read, worked, witnessed, but I'm far from what I would like to be and could be. I see how much I'm lacking. I've realized that I can't achieve everything I want to, so it's time, both because of wisdom and material fatigue, to focus. We're talking about miles. And now I conclude that the quality of the workforce has significantly declined. There are no quality attitudes towards work, dedication, or the desire for self-improvement. There is, but it's focused on the result. There's no breadth there. And yet, on the other hand, if they've already focused on a specific activity, I don't see top professionalism in its execution. It's like a defensive football player who can't make a cross or can't shoot on goal. The essence of modern football is offensive defenders. The French showed and proved it with their domination of the national football team, and later all modern football coaches accepted it. I won't mention countless other examples that exist in basketball and all other sports. Come on, people, wake up!

In the mass television broadcasts that are now present with all cable operators, they have started to cover all sports events, no matter how important they are, which has reflected on the quality. We even have broadcasts without commentators. Let's now focus on the quality of the broadcasts, which is in a huge decline. Quantity should never be at the expense of quality. That could not have happened in the past century. What is the problem? Are there too many of them? Well, not the same people work all day long. Quality has declined everywhere. The same is with people in companies. And with players. I haven't become that good compared to others, I've just continued to take small steps forward, in accordance with my capabilities, just as I have done my whole life. What happened to those who were far ahead of me? They stopped. They stopped trying to improve. They got tired. They got bored. They got comfortable. They started working in good companies in good positions and fell asleep there. Earlier, their desire pushed them to catch up with the competition, everything motivated them. A couple of years have passed, and they have now stopped. It's not a problem that they've stopped, but they've started degrading their knowledge. It's not their fault. Such is the process. If you don't push yourself to be better, you will start to become worse. If they forgot that on their way up, that's legitimate. Couldn't anyone have warned them about it? They could have, but they didn't. They didn't want to or couldn't? Could they themselves have realized that necessity, that danger? Of course, they could have, but their environment had forced them not to stand out. They became satisfied with their position, their income, their place in society. Okay. Not everyone is eager to constantly improve. Some even get exhausted on that path. Well, we're all tired of all that, but the desire to be better than we currently are, perhaps, is what drives us to overcome life. To make our lives better by being better ourselves. For our children, for our neighbors' children, to look up to us. If the desire to be better doesn't move us, then, perhaps, fear should preserve us. If we don't swim, we'll drown!

The same goes for players, managers, and everyone else. Fight for the team, for the club, but first and foremost, fight for yourself. Fight every day. Fight in training sessions, in the game, from the first to the last whistle. Fight for every ball, for every inch of that pitch. Be the best version of yourself. Be who you are. The result of the game is not important, what matters is that you left your heart on the field.

I love those companies that have a practice of 'walking' their employees horizontally through the company, making them change several departments, from production to sales, from sales to marketing, and then taking them back to production. The breadth of knowledge and skills these people bring back to their original department is priceless. It is wrong to strive only for the top. Don't just run towards the goal. Often, on the way to success, you need to run sideways.

Unlearning

Charles Darwin once said that the learning process consisted of learning and unlearning. To learn something is not as difficult as to discard what was previously learned. That is why coaches do not like old players. That is why managers do not like older employees. First, they need to unlearn what they know, and then learn and that will take an eternity; but that is so full of stereotypes. Some old players may not have had a good environment in which they took their first steps. They have the potential, but they have not had the opportunity to demonstrate what is best in them. Simply put, they did not grow up and develop in an environment that would allow them to demonstrate their best qualities. They simply did not have the opportunity to prove themselves or show off. Are you the best manager in the world? If you are, then you have to find not only unpolished and unrefined diamonds but also the poorly polished ones. And why waste your time on them? Why not strike while the iron is hot? Because the potential of those older players is incredible. They can serve multiple purposes. They are more loyal, dedicated, and mature.

They can keep the team on the field. They provide stability in defense, sharpness in attack, and maturity in crucial moments. No, they don't run much, they run wisely. Every move they make is measured, precise, and, what is very important, they make incredibly few mistakes. But they demand respect. If they get it, they will be loyal to you because they know how to appreciate and respect those who respect them. Naturally, there are cheats and lazy ones. Are you the best manager? If you are, then your job is to sniff out such characters and not only quickly get them out of your ranks but never hire them again. That's why you're the best, right? That's your job. No, they don't have to be the ones who will one day shine in the sky of the most promising stars, but they can provide the young blood with the opportunity to hone their skills on the field with the best. To replace you exactly where you are unable to be, where they are out of your reach. To teach and guide them properly. Honestly speaking, it is extremely demanding to do that. They constantly have a reputation for being lazy, not wise. There is that too, but that's why you're here. As the best leader, to sniff out and get rid of such characters who are just posing.

It is easier to employ young people because they learn easier and faster, but working with them also bring its own challenges. Often, these young people are picky about their jobs, they don't want to do everything, and they are not mature enough to approach work seriously. And why would they? They are young. They want to have fun. They want to enjoy all the benefits that their age offers. Oh, the recklessness of the young! But they also have energy that oozes out of every pore, so much that it spreads around. So, connect them. Connect these young and experienced people. I've been saying this all along. It's not all black and white. Add some color. Build a team, not a nursing home or a kindergarten. Build it with the players you have while constantly looking for those who would join your team and fit in your vision best.

I remember when, during an important match in the semifinals of the city championship, the coach of the school futsal team told me not to enter the central part of the field, as I liked to mingle everywhere, and to stick to the left wing only. Considering that I had been scolded for a year for not listening to the coach, that day I decided to be obedient because it was an important game and not to deviate from the left sideline. I listened to the coach, proud of myself. He would surely praise me, but I realized that I wasn't participating in the game as I used to. Yes, I was just a kid, disobedient, stubborn, but now I was good. I listened, but something wasn't right. There were no timeouts in the game. Even the coach saw that something wasn't right. And there I was, like a fool. My friends, parents, my own and other kids'parents, were pushing me, encouraging me to participate more in the game. I also saw that something was not working well. The coach had told me so. So, what was wrong now? I went from one extreme to another. From complete misbehavior to blindly accepting new tasks without understanding their essence. From learning to unlearning. Well, that's not the way to go. You shouldn't erase everything you've done well before and start with a blank slate. That's not unlearning. You need to embrace new knowledge and combine it with old. That's how synergy starts to produce results. So, what was the problem? The reasons are almost always the same. Either the coach didn't convey the message correctly, or the player didn't understand it well. Simply put, either they're not capable of following or they're not suitable for delivering instructions, neither those who receive them nor those who give them. That's why good communication is essential. Ask all participants if they understood well, and make them repeat what was agreed upon. Yes, it sounds silly, but it's necessary. The prerequisite for any success is good communication. I'm not just talking about work or sports, but also about life and marriage. Habits are difficult to change. That's why one needs to be precise and persistent.

Uncle Darwin says that whenever a new idea came to his mind, he had a rule to write it down within thirty minutes, because his brain would reject it due to prior learning. If he didn't write it down, it would disappear as if it had never been there. The brain resists new things, whether they are good or bad. It won't accept them. This is inherent in every person, every employee, and every player on your team. It's natural. Teach them to think. Teach them to separate the important from the unimportant. Teach them how to prioritize. Teach them how to learn and how to forget.

Until You Make It

As one of my esteemed colleagues would say, 'Fake it until you make it'. That statement has always haunted me. I've felt perplexed. It's like a man faking an orgasm. Maybe it's too subjectively male-oriented point of view? I understand the need to have a firm attitude and not show your weaknesses, but pretending, that somehow has never sat well with me. I'm not saying that I don't know how to do it, but it's not honorable to me. How can you fake it on the field? I'm not talking about Italian and Latin American footballers who acted their way into the pitch. I have always hated those exaggerated performances. I've already said that's why I always liked to watch the Premier League. There, when you fall and pretend, everyone points a finger at you and calls you by your real name, a fraud. Don't do it!

How can you cheat the whole stadium? Everything is transparent there. Everything is visible as daylight. There's no room for fakers. You can immediately see who's who, who knows what, and how much. The market is merciless. It sees everything, knows everything, and forgives nothing, like a self-regulating process that separates the wheat from the chaff. How can you fake it here? It has always been a rule that you can't fake a faker. I don't mean that you have to be a faker to catch a faker, on the contrary, you have to be an excellent coach, an excellent manager, to immediately recognize a fraudster. Yes, it's getting harder and harder. They have started camouflaging. However, let's be honest, they've started to believe in their own fake stories so much that they've become accustomed to them. They've stopped respecting the opponent, and as soon as you underestimate the opponent, your guard drops, and you receive blows unprepared. The consequences will be visible very soon. This applies to everyone. You simply try less and less and become worse and worse. They started to believe that they were really good, the best actually. The power of autosuggestion really works.

There's the saying: fool me once, shame on you; fool me twice, shame on me. Now people allow themselves to be fooled countless times. Who's crazy here? How can cheaters be expected to put in more effort when the same story has worked countless times with the same people? They see it working and why change a recipe for success? So dear fraudsters, your craft requires improvement, otherwise the competition will eat you alive. Young fraudsters are diligently devising new models to surpass their more experienced colleagues who are resting on the laurels of their past successes. The old have forgotten their beginnings. Success came easily to some, uncalled for, and like in any business, luck played its part and instead of recognizing it, they still continue with the same pattern of success. They don't change their work algorithm. Inexperienced. Doomed to failure. And yet they are still here. There are still new customers who want to be deceived. The market is global, there's room for everyone. I have so many 'relatives' in the world who tragically ended up in Africa and left me with a huge inheritance. All that I had to do was to transfer some money to a guy in Nigeria, supposedly a lawyer, so that he could forward my inheritance. But a new generation is evolving. Emails are now changing, they're of better quality, more serious. Markets are being selected. The profile pictures of those contacting me are changing, they're better, more convincing. Now the 'family' leaving me an inheritance has migrated to Asia, so I'm getting millions from some lost relatives in China, Japan, South Korea. Bravo. Competition and the market have forced them to be more proactive. But still, it's not at a satisfactory level. I write to them, calling on their sales conscience, on their professionalism. That it has to be better, more convincing. There's no point in embarrassing the profession. I know it's hard, but they have to try harder. You always have to bring something new to your business.

I'm one of those people who could never tell the same joke twice in the same way. I don't know if anyone listens to me again when I say it. I have to change it. Even if I don't know that there are some in the audience who were already present during my last performance, I'm the one who listens to the joke again. I've bored myself. I have to change it. Speaking of actors, on any stage in life, they always change their performance. Theater actors, the top ones, have never played a play twice in the same way. They have to adapt, change, and improve it.

How does it go in business, in life? It goes as others see you. Don't confuse the attitude you should have when others observe you with pretending. Don't fake yourself in the role you play. It's good to live with the character you're playing, but if you like the character, you have to work on yourself to become the person you strive to be. You have to show yourself in a good light. You have to be the best. You have to look like it too. Appearance matters. People like to work with successful people, it's natural. Everyone likes to be in the company of charismatic, cheerful people, around whom they feel good and comfortable. Don't confuse the attitude you need to radiate with your current state. You may be broken, but in the eyes of others, exude confidence. Be aware of your flaws and work on minimizing them. Work on yourself every day. Practice. This will be good primarily for you, and after that, it will be good for your job as well. But don't lie to yourself. Don't mix lying with covering up shortcomings. Don't lie to your audience. It shows. You can overcome criticism, that's legitimate, but you can't promise them the earth. That will come due someday. Unless you took an advance and fled in an unknown direction. But even then, a bad reputation will follow you in the market, not to mention that justice will catch up with you if you live in a country with a functioning legal system, or maybe you'll end up in politics, and then all your sins will be magically forgiven. God moves in a mysterious way, but let's get back to honest people and sincere actors, fighters who have their performance on the field of life.

When someone asks you if you know how to do something, and you don't, say you do, then quickly start learning what you said you already knew. This has been paraphrased, said many times by the most prominent successful business people on the planet. This is absolutely true, and there is no debate about it. The problem arises if you start believing in what you said, don't start learning, and don't do enough to fulfill what you promised. Who are you lying to? It will work with fools and idiots, but not with serious business people. And you want to play with the best? There's no room for that. Those cunning players have been through thick and thin. You have to earn the right to sit with them at the table, and you won't have many opportunities to do so. Many people never experience this in their lifetime. Use that pitch, those five minutes of fame, to present yourself in the right light. Enchant them with your charisma. When you succeed, then comes the other part. Deliver on what you promised. Then you must be honest with yourself. You have to look at yourself in the mirror and identify all the things you need to fix and improve so that you can deliver what you promised, paying attention to the deadlines and the quality. There is room to falter, there is room to not deliver, but there is no room to cheat.

We all pretend. The audience is the opposite sex, teammates, employers, business partners, colleagues, we are all on that stage. Players are in the most difficult situation. Everything is visible from the stands. Fans will forgive their club for poor results, management will forgive a manager for a series of failures, but they will never forgive lack of effort and pretense. If everyone sees that you are giving your all to be better, to be the best, no one will say anything to you if you fail. And even if they do tell you something then, if they criticize you, just ignore them and look for a new environment. They don't deserve you in their ranks. Okay, sometimes you can try until exhaustion, but you're just not good enough. You're not, man, for that league. You won't need anyone to point that out to you. You'll be aware that you don't belong there. You'll leave on your own.

And, listen to this! According to all the world's studies, people believe those who lie to them!? Countless behavioral studies point to the fact that our harsh reality is illogical. In the 1950s, Solomon Asch proved through his experiments that people would agree with the opinion of the majority within a group no matter how wrong it was. The whole group of participants said that one line was longer than the other, even though it was clearly not, and the person in the experiment agreed with the majority decision, no matter how wrong it was. There were, of course, those who maintained their stance, but they were in the minority. If the vote for the decision was public, the percentage of agreement with wrong decisions was even higher. People were ashamed to publicly confront phonies. We accept the majority opinion regardless of whether we agree with it or not.

People rely more on the story and presentation than on the product itself. We are more willing to pay for a service if it is nicely packaged, rather than if it is given to us for free or at a low price. Violinist Joshua Bell played for free for 45 minutes in the subway, but only a few stopped and listened to him. He earned $32 for about an hour of playing music, and a few days earlier he filled Symphony Hall in Boston at an average ticket price of $100. The hall was packed. Okay, it's not the same target audience in the subway and Symphony Hall, but still, much is too much. If we promise a lot and appear convincing without having to prove our claims, people will trust us more. Classic 'I'm the best, I do it the best, when I make it, no one is stronger, better, or more beautiful than me' is when people trust us more. People have a need to be deceived. But let's put it differently. People will believe in someone who believes in themselves. Who has the right attitude. That's why people don't buy a product but the experience they had while buying that product. The seller instilled confidence in them, he knew how to sell them something. It's not a scam, it's the art of sales. I'm not talking about scammers here. People follow the crowd because when something is good for someone else, it will be good for me too. That's why we also look for confirmations online for a purchase. But that's human nature. That's why I'm not talking about the attitude you have when presenting yourself or your product. I'm not talking about presenting yourself on the market field, but about the abuse of it. You sell yourself as a top player and congratulations on the presentation, but let's see what you look like on the field. Presentation after presentation, let's see what kind of player we've bought. Show yourself.

Fake it until you make it is not about pretending, it's about not giving up. It will be a tough game. The opponent is demanding. Defend wisely and wait for your chance to score. Give it your all. Be focused on defense, be precise on offense. Carefully choose your battles and time your strength. Be wise. Don't forget that the club (company) is built on the foundations of the team. You, as a team member, regardless of the hierarchical position that you hold, must have honest communication within the team.

You must clearly and loudly communicate your strengths and weaknesses within that family circle, in order to set a strategy that will bring success. I intentionally talk from both the player's and coach's perspective at the same time. It's intertwined. That's the team. That doesn't mean you shouldn't raise combat readiness before the battle, but you can't give your soldier an empty gun and tell him it's loaded and ready to fire. You must be honest with yourself first, and then with your fellow soldiers. That means enduring all the blows, all the hardships and all the misfortunes until you succeed, all the challenges that everyday situations on the field bring you, all the unpredictable circumstances, all the disruptive factors, both external and internal. But, if there's anything worse than defeat, it's a dishonorable victory. Don't forget, you're not alone. All your teammates are there to share the burden you carry. You chose such players, colleagues, comrades, who are not only there when both successes and failures are achieved. Choose your partners carefully, choose for whom you play and whose jersey you wear. Choose, above all, to be humane, and success will come naturally. Don't worry.

Process and Progress

In my, I can freely say, rich career, I have worked for a large number of companies that were at different stages of development, and each carried a part of the specificity in its procedural development wherever it was in its business. I have worked for small, large, multinational companies, well, in all ownership and organizational structures. I have worked at all levels in the organization, from a trainee to a manager, and there were always some processes, and there were always lapses in them. Is 'lapse' too strong a term? Some procedures needed to be improved, adapted. Someone, certainly, needed to adapt them. The process changed. The initiative had to come from all employees, regardless of where they were on the hierarchical ladder. All the employees and the management had to contribute to improving the work of the team.

Often, nothing was done.' Does it work? It works. Then don't touch it'. A famous developer's statement when programming software. Yet rarely did anyone delve deeply into the essence of the process itself from which somewhat improved, if any at all, procedure needed to emerge, because it didn't even exist before. When creating a project, it was always necessary to create tons of documentation. The path from an idea to the final product is very complex and requires careful monitoring of every part of the production process. Somehow everything is made and eventually works. Sometimes it turns out to be phenomenal, but it often happens that it doesn't turn out exactly as we wanted. Sometimes it turns out worse, and sometimes several times better than the initial idea. And great, let's move on to the next project. Only the wise return to see what they have done, to analyze the entire process, in order to recognize the good things they have done and turn them into practice for future projects or to determine where mistakes were made, why they were made, and to incorporate that into the procedure so that it never happens again. But the speed of today's way of life has also affected the approach to work. We immediately jump to the next project and don't have time to retrospect on the previous one. Petty excuses for potentially big mistakes.

I can't help but say that I absolutely hate changing companies. I often use an example from my own life of a car I bought a few years ago. I talk about how I wouldn't change my wife since I don't need a new headache in life; I'm sick of changing jobs; and the car I bought I rarely use so it would be a shame to change it even though I should, because its time is up, and now I can't even do that. I have been stuck with that car for quite some time. And change is healthy. Mind you, I don't like changing jobs. That's crystal clear. It's so exhausting. New people, new energy, sometimes good, often not. I don't like changes, and I've changed nine companies in 20 years?! Contradictory? No. I changed some because I wanted to, and some because it was necessary. The point is that there's no excuse for the status quo. There's no excuse for not constantly improving and perfecting yourself. I don't have the luxury of waiting for something to change on its own. I have to be the one to take action. Change towards progress must start with me. It's hard, often painful, but necessary.

In a huge company I worked for, one of the most prestigious and most inflated possible, the procedures became so entrenched that it was not seen, or intentionally ignored, and I never even wanted to get into that, that the profit calculator wasn't working. When I demystified their 'calculator' for calculating the not-so-complicated process of making a profit, because I couldn't just accept it as given since I had to understand it first, we realized how poorly the company was doing thanks to the headquarters. Completely non-transparent, and the process had to be completely transparent, which no one had questioned for years. The goal wasn't to rub someone's nose in it, but to identify all the parameters that affect business. The result was a revision of the contract.

To improve the process, you first have to understand it, and usually it's that story of how it's always been done that way and why change it now. You have to make an effort to understand why it was done that way in the first place. Accept the processes, procedures, and practices, of course. Start working according to them. First and foremost, understand the process, and then, if you see room for improvement, contribute. Be part of the company. Smart companies encourage and reward this approach to work. They encourage this way of working. But do you always have to be rewarded when you do something good? Doesn't it fill you with a sense of satisfaction when you improve and make your own and others' work easier?

In another multinational company I had the privilege of working for, and which was, remains, and will always be the greatest ever for me, the products sold so well on their own that lethargy in the sales process began to spread throughout the company, which was unprepared for new moves by the competition. The basics, which everyone was aware of, were neglected. The lessons learnt were not being renewed and they began to be forgotten. It was necessary for the balance of power on the market to be significantly disrupted for the company to wake up and become aware that the problem was already in its own yard. It identified the problem and began to solve it. Was it too late? No. It's never too late. But it was too painful. To this day, the company has not been able to regain the market share it had ten years ago. It didn't have to be that way. It will be able to regain it, but if it doesn't learn from this lesson what not to do in the future, then all this effort will have been in vain.

All of this is a completely natural process. People become inert. I intentionally say "become" because it is not natural. By nature, people push boundaries, explore, grow, and develop. And then, I suppose, they get tired? I would rather say that there are other reasons that influence such a person's decision. I immediately think of Karl Marx and his teaching that the means of production create man's consciousness. A person gets lost in everyday life. They forget their reason for existing. No matter how strange that may sound to you, you have to participate in your own life. It's yours, after all. No one can live it for you or take care of everything for you. The environment in which a person works, the team in which a player plays, largely determine the consciousness of the employee. The way the game is played, the approach to clients, the approach to the job by teammates, by managers, determine the consciousness of the worker. This is also a multi-layered process. Cause and effect. As important as team management is, so is the encouragement you receive from your teammates. If, in that fight, you can rely on your teammate, success is guaranteed. When the defense does their part, the attack will be more efficient and effective. Remember, you are all part of one team. The team consists of units which, as independent as they may seem, are not. This applies to a team as well as to a company (club), to anything, to any living organism. If one organ is not functioning well in the organism, other organs will suffer because of it. Everything is interconnected. You cannot fail to exercise, eat unhealthily, fail to take care of your body and soul, and then ask for maximum effort and engagement from it on the battlefield. Injury will occur immediately if there was no proper warmup. If you consume too much fat, your heart won't function properly. If you don't take care of the state of your mind, your brain will begin to disobey. The organism, the team, the company will begin to collapse like a house of cards. You won't notice it immediately. The organism is young and strong, but suddenly everything will start to fall apart. Employees will start to disobey and refuse to do their part of the job. Not because they don't want to work, but because they won't be able to. Then it won't be a matter of choice; it will be inevitability. Stark reality.

Communication can be a very tricky category. Rules of behavior can be stumbling blocks, stifling the creative process of work, beauty and playfulness of the game. They can undermine the atmosphere in the team, hinder the better development of each individual and trip up the entire team on its path to victory. Oh, sure. When you're building a team, it's like building a house. You need architects, builders, infrastructure, and materials. You need, of course, a construction plan. Just as a plan is necessary for building a house, it is also necessary for building a team and a company. However, when building a house or buying a car, for which you need to consult with your wife, here it is taken as a mitigating circumstance, so that you have one thing to worry less about in the company. Although, on second thoughts, you just need to listen to your wife and everyone's happy, and here you have freedom of choice, which can cost you dearly. Here you have to take responsibility for your decisions. Oh, despair. Tricky, but hey, we have to work in accordance with our life and business roles. To begin with, you need a plan. Any plan. It's better to have a bad plan than no plan at all. Write it down. Start creating according to that plan. Build on it. Let your process be iterative, but also incremental. Build your team the same way. When you've done that, who's stopping you from changing it later? It's normal to change and improve it. You've built a house, seen that something wasn't quite right and that you screwed up somewhere, so change it later. Improve, enrich, enhance. This isn't about mistakes, but about learning and improving the process, product, or service based on experiential actions you've gone through in the process itself. Look back. Do a retrospective of the events. It's in human nature to have to look back and see the work behind. Glory to Zoran Radmilović, a Serbian actor known in the cinematic history of former Yugoslavia for some of the most memorable roles.

It doesn't matter what size a company is or where it is on its development path. Whether it has been around for centuries or is a startup from a few years ago, the philosophy is the same. You have to fight every day and give your best every day to become wiser and better. And without a documented work process, it's hard to do anything right. That's why I started writing this, not because of my age, but because I am overwhelmed by a huge amount of different information, so in this sea of data and responsibilities, I'm trying to steer my boat through the waves.

And when you establish procedures and everything goes smoothly and everything starts to be magical, should you stop? No way. There's no room for stopping. You have to keep up with them, change them, adapt to new situations. The company must have a cop who will take care of everything, but it must also have someone who breaks boundaries, brings new perspectives, someone who brings fresh blood. Someone who thinks out of the box.

Inspirer

They say it's not possible to make someone both proactive and creative. It is difficult, but not impossible. The only way is to create such conditions, such a working environment in which people will motivate themselves. It's an extremely challenging task. Yes, it is. Many managers give up on motivating people, thinking that it is enough to occasionally give a motivational speech and that they have solved the problem. Now everyone is motivated because they have managed to transfer their energy through that speech. The reality is different. Setting up a creative environment that motivates employees is a process that requires absolute dedication at every moment, at every step, and in all areas of business. And yes, that's the micro-management that needs to be done. Don't deal with individual problems that can be solved at the level at which they arise, but constantly listen to the way the company is breathing. Every breath, every moment is important. The beauty is in the small things because they usually hide big answers and signs that we must follow on the path to success. I just want to remind you of the theory of motivation or Herzberg's two-factor theory. It is based on the idea of exploring, finding, and defining factors that contribute to job satisfaction or dissatisfaction. According to Herzberg, there are two groups of factors - one that leads to employee satisfaction and another that can prevent dissatisfaction. That's why we have motivational factors and hygiene factors. Use them correctly and in line with the goals you want to achieve. Be aware that they are always there. Take care of what needs to be fulfilled to satisfy the basic conditions for smooth work execution and what motivates your fellow fighters.

People should be enabled to be creative. This does not mean giving them tools such as computers, desks, and chairs, but providing an environment that exudes success and a desire to be better and more dedicated. Listening to these employees, recognizing their desires and aspirations, and enabling them to achieve their goals, both professionally and personally. A satisfied player will also be satisfied when they can provide something for themselves, and the next step is when they start to provide support to others. It is in human nature to help. Finally, by helping ourselves, we also help others. To be able to recognize, one must first learn to observe. And that is learned. I observe my children and see that they have a propensity for art, specifically painting and music. Aha! I saw, noticed. I looked at what I could do to help. I brought a mini keyboard for my son, borrowed it from a friend and paid for online music lessons, while for my daughter, I arranged for private painting lessons. Let's be clear, I don't have a desire for them to pursue music or painting. I'm trying to help them develop their creative side. To be richer in their knowledge and experience that will enrich them as people. So, the first thing is done. Potentials, interests, possible aspirations are recognized. The second step is providing the conditions for them to practically master those skills and knowledge. The third step, they don't like it because it's too difficult or they're so interested that they forget all their other responsibilities. These are some of the possible scenarios that have happened many times before. If they give up on that path, which is a very common case, and you see that they are good at it but it's just too hard, give them encouragement to persevere. Give them a tangible, realistic goal to strive for. Don't force them, they may not want to go that way at all. And if they go too deep and forget their other responsibilities, remind them that besides the creative side, a person also needs the boring, functional side. Mundane responsibilities cannot be neglected.

Does this only apply to those at the beginning of their careers? Is there an age limit? Absolutely not. Let me give you another personal example. Some acrylic paints and a canvas from my daughter's painting classes were stashed away, forgotten. It was time to either use them or throw them away. The paints have already started to dry. My wife started cleaning the house, of course, on the first sunny spring day of the year when we all needed to spend some quality time outside in nature. Household chores had to be done. I respect that. I told her not to throw away the paints, but to take them and paint something on the canvas. We needed a picture for the living room, and I had been trying to convince her for a long time to embellish that wall with one of her works. She wanted to buy a painting, but we couldn't find the time for that, as we needed to choose it together since we would enjoy it together. Still, I kept pointing out that it would be the most beautiful and best if she painted something with her own hands. It would be more beautiful and more precious because it was the work of her own hands. I didn't give up on that idea because she had told me earlier that she loved to paint as a child. And after a few years of persuasion, that was the moment when my persistence finally had to yield results. She succeeded! Or rather, we succeeded. A beautiful painting emerged after a few days of her artistic creation. Another creative side of her personality turned into a beautiful painting that still occupies a central place on the wall of our living room. And it didn't stop there. She didn't stop at just one painting, but continued to create. The fact that certain parts of our apartment now resemble a studio, and that the apartment is filled with the smell of turpentine, is now less important. Or rather, I got what I was looking for. We discovered where our daughter's inclination for painting comes from. Goal set. Plan for achieving the goal adopted. Resources secured.

Obstacles overcome. Result achieved, even surpassed in multiple dimensions.

The initiators are different. Different. They depend on the sensitivity of the individual. There is no universal initiator as there is no universal solution. It all depends on the person. The only constant in all of this is your desire to pursue it. You are the pillar of all change. You as a manager, you as an employee. The flame of the desire to be better must not be extinguished. If it does, it's hard to reignite it. It does eventually ignite, of course, but the job is much harder and more complicated. You need to build momentum again. Like with a car. It's easy to go from 100 km/h to 160 km/h, but how much was needed to go from a standstill to 100 km/h? Why do motor vehicles have the most power in the lower gears? Well, that's why.

Your task is to lead them, to help them take those first steps. As Zarathustra said, 'Soon the torrents will come, and I will be your dam, your support on that path. Grab onto me, whoever can, but remember one thing, I am not your crutch'. Help them as if they were a young sapling by being the support that helps them strengthen at the beginning. That's when they need help most, but after that, their path is their own and you can only guide them later, without being a training wheel on their bike. Or, if they completely neglect their responsibilities and move away from their regular activities, you must bring them back, direct them. That's the manager's job, to lead them through that process. If everything goes well, they will be better and more prepared for new challenges on a professional and personal level. They will be richer and better people. But what if it doesn't go well? What if it was just wasted time and money? So what? You tried, you started, you motivated. It's clear that you care, that you're creating an environment that may produce something better. You've understood your team, seen their sensibility. You've seen what they're made of, what motivates them, and what doesn't. No one guarantees success, but that realization shouldn't deter you from wanting to be better and doing everything in your power to do something, to make a change.

Giants

No matter how much I appreciate and respect Sir Alex Ferguson, who marked my childhood and significantly influenced my mindset with his testimony of a work model, Mr. Brian Clough holds a special place in my heart and soul. Brian Clough's story always finds me when I need it most. It constantly motivates me to overcome myself. No matter how many times I've encountered it, I always find something that I need at that particular moment. I won't remind you of his successes, but I have to mention something, for my own sake. You take over a faltering Derby County and finish that year in the 18th position in the Second Division. The following year, you not only save it from relegation but also make it a team that wins that Second League, and then enters the First League and wins one of the most prestigious football championships in the world, the English League, and in the process, reaches the semi-finals of the UEFA Cup. Then they kick you out of that Derby County, well, you get yourself out of it with your youthful-rebellious ideology, although I'd prefer to call it stubbornness. Then you make a huge mistake and take over a club that you don't respect, Leeds United, hoping to satisfy your ego, instead of choosing an environment that will appreciate and respect you. They kick you out of there like the last bum because you've deserved it. You went where you knew you wouldn't be respected. And then you take over Nottingham Forest, which was in the Second League. You qualify with it for the English Premier League and win it for the first time in club history. And then you win the most prestigious club competition in the world, now known as the Champions League, not once, but twice in a row.

It is said that innate charisma, determination towards success and an unscrupulous approach in achieving the goal are characteristics of all the greatest ones. Sir Alex Ferguson is said to have known the name of everyone in the club, from the janitor to the head of the board of directors. He knew how to address everyone and devote a part of his time to them. Such a story also follows Bill Campbell. However, the point is not in their incredible memory capacity for registering such details, but in their understanding of how important it is to respect each individual of that great corporate organization, because each of them, regardless of where they are on the hierarchical ladder, makes their invaluable contribution to the functioning of that corporate organization. You show them respect because they deserve it. Another thing that characterizes all of them is that they knew how to use not-so-gentle language in their daily communication. Yes, passion is also expressed through communication. And communication, verbal or written, must be exactly the way a person experiences it. Harsh, sharp, honest.

Many did not want to hang out with those giants and have drinks with them, but everyone wanted those people to lead them through business, through life. Brian Clough used to say, 'Show me a man who thinks everyone loves him, and I'll show you a man who's mistaken'. It is impossible for everyone to love you. Were they some kind of 'good' dictators? No. They were just brutally honest. They were always criticized for building awe, which is not really true. They spoke of this themselves. How can a frightened person give their best? They can't. Instead of instilling awe, they built respect. This process could not have been done without sincere and open communication, but it had to be known who had the final saying in that process. Don't instill awe, but respect based on authority and credibility.

Control and discipline were key factors in their work. But they themselves were not agents of change, they were only switchmen and catalysts. They created conditions and an environment to make positive changes possible. Changes come from people themselves. You can't force people to be better just by wanting or saying they need to be. You have to dedicate yourself to them. The essence is in the details. You have to have an eye and a sense for the little things that affect every aspect of business. You have to understand how people breathe. This process inevitably creates new leaders. Leaders create leaders. How many successful managers have emerged by learning from these giants? As they themselves say, the key is not in the power that a leader has, but in control. The control over others, but above all control over themselves. Leadership is a balance of listening, learning, and leading. They were always dedicated to their work. Through their work, they set an example for others. They were the first to come and the last to leave work.

Many top football managers were not top players, but that was not the case with Brian Clough. He was an exceptional player, but his playing career ended prematurely due to an unfortunate accident. He scored 251 goals in 274 matches. He transferred his philosophy of the game to his managerial job. Swaying football was played, for the audience, for the client. He was good at assessing a player's personality and bringing out the best in him, making him better than he was at that moment.

He showed confidence, but he was also vulnerable. The fact that these giants sometimes neglected their families is another story, but always make sure to be at the top of your game everywhere. When you give so much at work, there is a great danger that you cannot fully devote yourself to your own family at home. Unfortunately, energy is finite.

Be careful about that, too. Keep it in mind constantly. Yes, according to my philosophy professor, even Socrates was a terrible person, but he was one of the greatest, if not the greatest, contributors to philosophy, its founding father. But shouldn't you always be the same, everywhere and at any given moment? The path is exhausting. Make sure to recharge your batteries, as the drain is huge, strong, sudden, and the energy you give to others is not infinite; you also need to regenerate it.

Arm yourself with friends, because you can't walk that path alone. Brian Clough's success is not just his. Peter Taylor is equally responsible for his success. Oh, how difficult it is to find your comrade, wingman, sidekick. Someone who is next to the first, but without the ambition to be first. Almost impossible. You will find a leader sooner than a leader will find his assistant, who does not want, like Iznogoud, to become the sultan instead of the sultan. If you find him, don't forget to treat him like the most precious thing, because he gives you the strength for today and tomorrow. Show him respect, because without him, yesterday's successes would not have been possible, and the future ones are almost unattainable.

I want to be like Brian Clough. I want to be vulnerable. I want to be wise. I want to be charismatic. I want to be part of a team, not just to rely on myself. I don't care if I'll be appreciated by the people, whose opinions I don't give a damn about, regardless of the accolades they might offer. I want to feel at home at work. I want us all to live the same dream. I want to be better today than I was yesterday. I want to be better tomorrow than I am today. I don't want success at all costs. I want to feel passion each day. I want to make people feel inspired so that they can give their all at any given moment.

Silver Bullet

What do we have now? Celebrated managers who have changed the philosophy of the game and achieved results that are unattainable to many, and now they are struggling. Mourinho, Benitez... There are too many of them. Does that mean their systems weren't valid? Not at all. So how did they use to get results?

Everything changes. You have to constantly improve, upgrade, and change. Will that bring you success? Maybe yes, maybe no. Many things will have to fall into place for everything to turn out right. Atmosphere, team, luck, you. And still, nothing is guaranteed. That's what I'm talking about.

As I said in a conversation with a friend, 'It's important that we tell our children what is right and what is not and that we never give up on that story, but even more important is that we don't just pass it on to our children with words, but primarily with our actions. Let us do what is up to us, in the hope that they will someday remember, when they need it most, what we told them and that it will help them make the right decision'. It's important that everyone does their part. Children perform their part masterfully. They test boundaries, push them, and it's up to us to do our part well. Are we doing that well?

Extract the best from the situation you are currently in. Draw from the present. Look around you. Observe the everyday things, but now think about them a little more carefully and you may see something completely different. Maybe not right away. And that takes practice. Step back to see better. Even athletes when they start for the triple jump, long jump, or any discipline where they gain momentum, take a step back. Have you seen that? You have. You've seen it countless times, but now you're going to look at it a bit differently. It's the same with life. One step back is preparation for a big leap forward. It has to be that way. Give yourself space. Steady the ball. Assess the situation. Make room and go.

Everyday life and routine lead us into a dark forest, and there we can't see the forest for the trees. Focus, please. Be patient and you will see the chance, opportunity, possibility. A light break will give you strength, not to continue, but to be better. Just slowly. Step by step. It doesn't mean that sometimes you shouldn't speed up, run, jump, or land, but I'm saying that it's completely normal and desirable to sometimes slow down, stop, stand, squat, take a time out, and if necessary, go back a little.

We need a constant reminder that it's how it has to be. If you have the privilege of having someone next to you who will push, drive, and nudge you, then sometimes listen to them, and if you don't have that luck, then you're left to yourself and you'll have to root for yourself. Arm yourself with patience. Don't forget how long the journey from your butt to your head is and how many more obstacles there are on that path. First, you need to unlearn a lot of things so that you could gain new knowledge, habits, and then develop new skills.

Don't let others manipulate you. Don't deceive yourself into thinking that you can change the world. Powerful people are the ones who change and create the world. You can only change yourself. You can be better. And is there a more powerful person than the one who has managed to change himself through small victories and persistent effort? I bear witness to you who want to listen. I speak to those I want to; I speak to those I have to. I speak to my nearest and dearest, my friends, I speak to my children, and above all, I speak and repeat to myself.

Guitarist John Mayer, of whom Eric Clapton himself said was not aware of how good he was, explained one of his compositions. He explained it not to show how to play it, but to help people understand it. To understand the music itself. He pointed out that you could play his song fantastically, but if you didn't break down the entire composition into its constituent parts, you wouldn't understand its essence because you could play anything in any way from its parts. You have to get into the melody to understand it. Disassemble it and then assemble it. You have to go to its source to know where it flows, and from the source, you can change its course. Find your own path, unique to you. You can't solve different problems with the same tools. Although challenges and problems are similar on your path to success, everything is different. You need to think out of the box to overcome everyday challenges. Don't let pride cloud your judgment. Don't let it become an obstacle for you. I know it's hard, but that's the only way. Step out of your comfort zone.

Trust also needs to be built. You must vouch your work. In ancient Rome, engineers who built a bridge would stand under it at its opening while people and vehicles crossed it. That's how credibility was built. That's how people trust you. Just as people have to trust you, you must work with people you trust. If you don't trust them, don't work with them.

Those same Romans didn't try to invent the wheel. They quickly realized the benefits of history. They adapted their gods to the same gods that the ancient Greeks had. They didn't change what worked. Don't dismantle the system from the root, although many people are prone to it.

Don't reinvent the wheel, but draw on the best of the past. Look back not to admire your successes or mourn missed opportunities, but to learn from your victories and defeats to gain wisdom for the future.

Accept reality whether you like it or not. Don't lie to yourself. Accept it and start building, creating on a solid foundation. Create slowly, in small steps. Focus on small victories because they will give you the will and strength to continue. And don't think about perfection. Nothing has to be perfect. Progress, not perfection, is the essence of every day, every moment. Don't think too much about missed opportunities or you will lose focus. Don't let your thoughts wander. This will save you time and energy. Choose your battles. Very often the key is in reducing costs rather than achieving higher sales. Remove what you don't want to get what you do. Only hit the balls you can hit. When the right opportunity comes, you will be ready and have the strength to seize that chance. Be patient and wise.

Have a plan, but don't forget Peter Drucker's words that culture eats strategy for breakfast. You must learn to adapt, which brings us back to Charles Darwin, who pointed out that in the ruthless battle of evolution and the market, it's not the strongest individuals that survive, but those that adapt to change the fastest. Find your niche. Specialize. Take a simple idea and take it very, very seriously. Even Tom Watson, CEO of IBM, said he's not a genius, but he's highly specialized. He's smart about certain things and sticks to them. You can't know everything and be the best at everything. Know your limits and capabilities. Play it safe. Play for yourself.

There is no silver bullet. There is no sure formula for success. Not everything can be measured and quantified. There are no laboratory conditions in real life. Something in small quantities can be beneficial, but in large quantities, it can be disastrous. Always ask yourself why you're doing something. Investigate inconsistencies. And never forget Friedrich Schiller's words that the voice of the majority is not the proof of correctness. Be yourself.

Many professors at the world's most prestigious universities try to decipher the recipe for the success of these giants. Many wise people are searching for a model of successful business. Whether they will be able to share that formula with the rest of the world, if they ever get to it, I cannot say. What I can conclude at this moment is that the key is in the details. First and foremost, you must show empathy towards your fellow combatants. You must treat them not as resources to achieve your desired goals, but as people, which they are. You must give them the attention and care they deserve. Communication is also crucial. It must be honest and open, both when talking to others and especially when talking to yourself. The passion you carry must not only carry you, but also be transmitted to others. Perseverance and consistency in what you do must exist at every moment, at every step, no matter how heavy the burden may be. Special emphasis is placed on respect. You must respect others. You must respect your friends, but also those who are not, and above all, you must respect yourself.

In the end

Thanks to Tim Berners-Lee. Thanks to open knowledge databases that are available to all of us. Thanks to all the good and not so good teachers. Thanks to all the victories and defeats. Thanks to all those wonderful people who selflessly share their ideas, knowledge, and experiences with the whole world. Thanks to all the wise. Thanks to all those sturdy, humble human giants. Thanks to all those who dared to share their life stories with all of us. Thanks also to all those who gave me strength and support. Thanks to all my friends and to all those who are not. Thanks for all the perspectives and all the unspoken words. Thanks to all the documentaries, feature films, and animated movies. Thanks for every book I've read and those waiting to be read. Thanks for every new day and every chance. Thanks for every breath and every moment. Thanks to all the writers. Thanks to all the participants in my everyday life. Special thanks not to one, not to two, but to three Milošes: Miloš Zlatanović, who unknowingly urged me to finish the book, Miloš Grozdanović, a Serbian writer who helped me shape its literary contours, and Miloš Arandjelović for the filigree details, which were, to be honest, not exactly filigree. Immense thanks to my family for absolutely everything. Thanks to all these giants on whose shoulders I observe the world.

Afterword

The psychology of professionalism or how to understand modern world of business

The moment primates started to differentiate as a separate branch of mammals, some 85 million years ago, is viewed as the starting point of development, of brain cells above and before everything. In a young primate, the brain structures take up 12% of the body mass, whereas in other mammals it is just 6%. The visual cortex makes for the biggest part of the brain mass. Its task is to process and integrate visual stimuli, that is, information. This means that we are born to observe things and that visual information is the most significant to us. Naturally, the essence of the visual perception and apperception is a movement. Ever since the first football club was formed in England on October 26th, 1863, kicking the ball and the perception of this game (i.e. watching it) has become the most important of all unimportant things in the world.

What is the purpose of the world of business and money? What determines when the goal will be scored or who will score three points in basketball or who will reach the finish line first? Is there a rule in such arbitrary situations? If there is, it can be found in this book. It goes without saying that it does not provide instant solutions; yet it offers the possibility to ask yourself the following question 'Where am I now and where do I go from here?' and then answer it. The world might be a cruel place, a cruel game; there might be a lot of defeated players and just a few winners. But who determines this? Certainly not our immediate surroundings but the way we live in it. How to achieve success as an individual who manages or wants to manage a team in the world of business? You don't need to be a horse to teach people how to ride.

If you want to have a successful team, then each individual needs to have their own place, but that particular place must be determined by the manager.If the manager cannot find the appropriate place for the team members, then those people are just excellent professionals in a dysfunctional team. In such an environment, not even Messi can lift the Champions League trophy even though he is one of the best Barcelona players. The manager needs to be a prophet in their position; they must notice small discrepancies in what is being done, to foresee that Verstapen will overtake Hamilton because he is driving in his own lane. Each team member needs to run their own race; some might be as fast as a cheetah and some miles behind the prey, just like hyenas. If you ask a cheetah to do hyena's work, then you are on the right path to destroy your team.

There is no instant success, and, as the author mentions in the book, Sir Alex Ferguson managed to win the first Champion's Title 7 years after he had taken over Manchester United. It appears that somebody wanted to be a cheetah on their own. Why do people crave the moment of glory? Why do they chase after instant success and instant solutions? The wish to fulfill the narcissistic goal of becoming a star is often followed by an immediate failure right after the glorious moment has passed. One good book does not necessarily mean the Nobel prize for literature.

If you lead a small team, it doesn't mean that you can't succeed; it just means that you need to make each team member do literally everything that the coach has told them to do. Famous Dragiša Binić, according to an urban legend, had the task to outrun the opponent quarterback ten times during the game with Bayern in Munchen. He achieved that and Red Star (Crvena Zvezda) scored two goals as a guest and beat the great Bayern right in the middle of Munchen after all the centershots.

As a manager, you need to feel each team member's emotion at the right time, you need to see beyond the obvious. So how come does the best person suddenly, almost overnight, become their antipode? If you succeed in understanding your subordinates, then you will be understood on both verbal and emotional scales. It is said that a good manager knows their players like the back of their hand. People generally feel better when they are heard and understood. It is a reciprocal process and the one who gives closeness and the sense of belonging. receives those in equal amounts.

We live in the time of powerful people and their subordinates. The ultimate virtue is to possess the ability to adapt. Jung says that the foundation of such behavior is in the tzar archetype since you bow your head when you approach the tzar and walk backwards when you leave him. Tzar's mercy is the greatest gift, and the quality and virtue are in humility and obedience. And yet, the world has always been improved by genius people who almost never felt the benefits of their own work. It might be a curse of simply the law of the pack. If you stand out too much, you will be cut down to size, for your own mistake and as an example to others not to do what you have tried. Even Galileo obeyed the law but at the very end he said 'And yet it moves.' The point might be to believe in yourself even when nobody understands you or even when they reject you.

You need to be persistent, some will argue, as Germans are in football; you need to play until the very end even when it is the first time you have played in your life. When asked by a potential employer whether he could work on assembling a car engine in the BMW factory, a friend of mine said 'Of course, I can!' even though he had never seen an engine before. Once we have overcome the fear of ourselves, we discover the potential of, to put it in Andrić's words, 'Everything that we could have been and could have done'. Serbian spite, some will say, even to our own detriment. A story goes that there is a company in Canada with a sign that says, 'If you are Serbian, consider yourself hired!' They say that some crazy Serbs saved the company from demise. How did they manage to do it? Very simple, actually. They decided to work without any remuneration until the company became solvent again. Crazy or even crazy and brave at the same time! Yet those same Serbs beat themselves in football. How come? Well, they don't play until the end. They can make sense out of absolutely nonsensical situations, but they cannot remain organized even when they are winning. So it is really questionable if Zare always plays until the very end.

The greatest victory is won when you give up on something else. When you offer someone a freedom of choice. Suddenly they lose their support, everything becomes more complicated since it is always easier to have someone to lead the way. Britain conquered India the moment it gave it its freedom.

The 'It Girl' or 'Golden Boy' syndrome always poses the question of the ability to choose or to deal with ambivalence. Buridan's donkey died of hunger because he couldn't decide where the grass was greener. Making decisions is a huge problem if there are options which are equally or almost equally appealing. When you need to choose between two pretty girls, it is usually the third one who hasn't even been in the game. The more decisive, the rudest wins; the indecisive one becomes the donkey. We always make the right choices even when we think we could have done better. What we don't know is that we choose unconsciously, but in accord with our own inner self, with the collective and personal unconscious. That's why we don't need to dread the decision-making process because all our decisions are always the right ones. Some will say that you can never know what good it may bring. It goes without saying that the more capable you are, the better the performance, resourcefulness, and the ability to understand and make decisions are. Smart businessmen used to send their children to other businessmen's companies so that they would learn what it was like to work for someone else. It was an excellent way for their sons to learn how to treat others and not to be vain and audacious.

Nowadays it has become popular to use the word onboarding for introducing new workers into the company. As babies we all survived onboarding. Not all of us were loved and wanted. Some were ignored and left aside. They didn't get enough support nor attention. They became attention seeking, dependent on the approval of others, which could never compensate for the lack of the initial one.Such people were paralyzed from an early age, never growing up to be mature enough to take on new challenges.

Vain wealthy people take very young children to shape them into successful people. They usually end up as unsuccessful great talents, never fully accomplished nor ready to accept their roles if they are ever given ones. Ottoman Turks had special military infantry units, known as the Janissary, recruited from the abducted infants of the enslaved peasants (usually from Bosnia and Serbia but also from other Balkan regions). They turned those children into cold-blooded assassins, the conquest machines. The first thing they took away from them was a sense of origin. They erased their past, their emotions and created merciless warriors.

It is said that being a parent is the most challenging task. No one is prepared for that. It just happens and we do our best. We are successful provided we have lots of love and patience. Not always, though. The integration of experience and youth can function if there is love and understanding. It is never just ratio. All our memories are saved as the unity of the situation and the accompanying emotion. Nothing is without emotions. Good parents are the ones who allow emotions to govern their families. Even those who argue and fight are somewhat better than the ones who are empty and cold. Children learn emotions from us. They need to be taught both positive and negative ones so that one day they could distinguish between them. You don't need to protect children from emotions. We are all mistaken when we think we shouldn't be talking about difficulties. Actually, children endure difficult situations better. If you want a good associate, let them express their emotions freely; let them cry when they are sad, allow them to express anger. In that way they will learn how to control their emotions and become mature in the process. That's why Matt Busby was right when he believed in children, being the father figure who was not shielding them from difficulties but provided support when it was needed.

Finally, it's all about becoming mature, that is, learning and unlearning. It has to do with accepting mature and adaptable models and rejecting the immature, distracting ones. The thing is in making progress, in mastering mature skills. Nula dies sine linea is the key to success. You can always reach the next level, you can always make progress. Therefore, the young should be allowed to make mistakes, to reject immature patterns, to cry for the unattained goals and to adopt the mature decisions they will eventually make themselves. The meaning of life is in moving forward, not in standing still. Dragonfly has just one day of life and a purpose to leave offspring, another dragonfly that will have just one day of life. The meaning is in living life and becoming mature, from the cradle to the grave. Those are the two ends in which existence is identical. Death is the foundation of life and life is the foundation of death, another dragonfly.

At the very end, if you wish to know the way the world of business and a good team with a good manager functions, you should read this book. You will understand the way modern humanity works, and if you say that everything was better in the olden days, you will realize that this is the best time, that it is always the best time to make progress and become mature. The author of this book rightfully reminds us that football is the most important of all unimportant things in the world. Recently, I've read a SciFi story about football being the most lucrative business on this planet and that some really important issues, even the political ones, revolve around it. The author managed to get to the jist of it and transferred it onto the paper, in an exquisite, inspired and poetic way.

This book is for those who still have the thirst for progress in them, who haven't yet been swallowed by the snake king, who believe in empathy and love, who stargaze, and don't want to be owned and imprisoned in the golden cage. As Antoine de Saint-Exupéry' Little Prince said to the rose, 'I will always love you' 'No', said the rose, 'One day I will wither and then no one will admire me' 'That's strange', answered Little Prince, 'If you were mine, I would love you even then.'

Dragan Milošević, MD specialist, psychiatrist, psychotherapist

Bojan Mladenović
Play That Game

Editing and Proofreading
Miloš Aranđenlović,
Jovan Marinković,
Miloš Zlatanović,
Milos Grozdanovic

Makeready
Milos Grozdanovic

Cover Design
Miloš Zlatanović

English Translation
Nina Ranđelović

Niš, Serbia 2023
playthatgamebook@gmail.com
www.playthatgame-book.com